THE TRIPLE GEM

THE TRIPLE GEM:

AN INTRODUCTION TO BUDDHISM

by

GERALD ROSCOE

SILKWORM BOOKS
Chiang Mai 1994

First published in 1994 by
Silkworm Books
54/1 Sridonchai Road, Chiang Mai 50100, Thailand

Silkworm Books is a registered trade mark of Trasvin Publications Ltd., Part.

National Library of Thailand Cataloguing in Publication Data
Roscoe, Gerald
        The Triple Gem: an introduction to Buddhism
        1. Buddhism   I. Title
        294.3
        ISBN 974-7047-27-6

Design by T. Jittidejarak
Cover painting by Prasong Tongtawat
Set in 11 pt. Palatino by Silk Type

Printed in Thailand by O.S. Printing House, Bangkok

CONTENTS

PREFACE

This work is subtitled "An Introduction to Buddhism" and it is just that, an introduction, intended primarily for the Western reader seeking a simple, concise, easy-to-read guide to the Buddhist way of life. It incorporates, with revisions and additions, my three previous books about Buddhism, each of which dealt with one of the Three Jewels of what is called Buddhism's Triple Gem. One of those Jewels is the Buddha, the founder of Buddhism. Another is the *Dhamma*, the teachings of Buddhism. And the third is the *Sangha*, the monastic order of Buddhism.

The form of Buddhism discussed in this book is Theravadan, especially as practiced in Thailand, where Buddhism is the state religion and where there is but a small Muslim minority and an even smaller Christian minority among the approximately sixty-five million Thai nationals.

Theravadins regard their Buddhism as the Way of the Elders, which is the very meaning of Theravada, and as directly derived from the teachings of the Buddha as recorded in the earliest written texts, the Pali Canon. Theravada, called by some the Old Wisdom School, by others Hinayana (the Lesser Vehicle), is the Buddhism of Southern Asia — Thailand, Burma, Cambodia, Sri Lanka — whereas Maha-yana (the Greater Vehicle), a later form, is

the Buddhism of northern Asia — Tibet, China, Japan
(Zen), Mongolia, Korea. (Some residents of Thailand
practice Mahayana Buddhism, especially some Chinese
monks and their followers, and some Vietnamese.)
    Buddhism is moving westward — there are now
more than half a million Buddhists in North America (1992)
— and whether it is practised in any of its various permutations — Theravada, Mahayana, Vajrayana (the Diamond
Vehicle), Zen, Tao-combined — the permutations are less
important than the "refuge" that all Buddhists find in The
Triple Gem.

******

Pali is the ancient literary language of Theravada Buddhism — and remains to this day its ecclesiastical language.
(Sanskrit is the language of Mahayana Buddhism). Because
many Pali words cannot be translated literally into English
circumlocutions must be used. There are many translated
versions of the Buddha's discourses; some are rendered in
remarkably beautiful, though perhaps somewhat fanciful,
formal language, others in awkward, archaic, and all too
often incomprehensible language.
    Fortunately, the meaning of what the Buddha said, if
not his exact words, may be ascertained from the best of the
various translations and circumlocutions, and it is to the
meaning that I have turned when citing lines from the
Buddha's discourses, the *suttas*, or other portions of the
Buddhist scriptures. Furthermore, I have rendered them in
contemporary language in order to make the Buddha's
teachings more accessible and meaningful to today's readers.
    I have used Pali terminology where appropriate to the

text except in those instances where Sanskrit words are more familiar to Westerners. For examples, *nirvana* and *karma* are Sanskrit, words more familiar to Westerners than their Pali counterparts, *nibbana* and *kamma*. The glossary in the Appendix lists words in both their Pali and Sanskrit forms.

******

I have been living in Thailand, a Buddhist land, for many years, studying and following the path of Buddhism. I have learned that Buddhism is not authoritative, not ritualistic, not speculative, and not metaphysical; that it abjures divination, superstition, and soothsaying; that it is democratic, without prejudice and bigotry; that it is therapeutic and pragmatic, a way of life.

I have also learned that this remarkable religion does not believe in praying to a divinity, ignores the question of whether there is a God, and discourages reliance on ritual and ceremony. Instead, Buddhism teaches one to rely on oneself and to find truth within oneself.

"Look within," the Buddha said, "for thou art Buddha."

Gerald Roscoe

PART I

THE DHAMMA

CHAPTER ONE

THE APPEAL OF BUDDHISM

More than five hundred centuries older than Christianity, one of the great, enduring religions of Eastern civilization, Buddhism is today finding new sources of strength and vitality in the Western world.

Increasingly, throughout Europe, Great Britain, Australia, North America and elsewhere, men and women in search of meaningful lives are being attracted to Buddhism, often motivated at first by intellectual curiosity and then finding a deeply gratifying personal nourishment.

As the French expression has it, "Je suis athéiste mais Catholique", it may be said by many Western practitioners, "I am Christian but Buddhist", or "I am Jewish but Buddhist." It certainly may be said, "I am atheist but Buddhist", for Buddhism concerns itself with human, immediate, practical matters rather than whether there is a God.

It's worth noting that an acceptance of Buddhism does not necessarily require a rejection of one's parental or earlier-life religion. In fact, Buddhism does not *require* anything of those who would practice it. For Buddhism is not dogmatic nor catechistic. It does not preach sin. It does not say there is only *one* right way. It offers merely a path to wisdom, to enlightenment; the very word Buddha derives from *buddh*, to be awake, to be enlightened. The Buddha, the Fully Enlightened One, was a human being, not a divinity, a human being who was above all a teacher.

What the Buddha taught—what is known as the *Dhamma*[1] —might be described as how to live the good life. This is what he taught monks and nuns and laypersons (who in the Buddha's time were referred to as householders, a term used by monks yet today.) For both monastics and laypersons, living the good life—a life of morality, meditation, and the cultivation of insight- wisdom—would lead, the Buddha taught, to enlightenment and *Nirvana*, two concepts quite difficult for the Western mind to embrace and which I will explain further on.

Buddhism offers **a way of life** which in many ways is not dissimilar from that offered by Christianity, Judaism, Hinduism, Islam, Confucianism, Taoism, or any of the world's religions—and in many ways is. The similarities between Buddhism and other religions lie in their approach to morality. The Christian-Judaic commandments. The Islamic code. The Vedas and Upanishads of the Hindus. The Buddhist precepts.

For the Buddhist layperson there are five precepts: "I undertake the rule of training to refrain from" (1) destroying life, (2) taking what is not given, (3) illicit sexual relationships, (4) false speech, and (5) intoxicants causing heedlessness. (These precepts will be further discussed in subsequent chapters.)

---

[1] Throughout this text *Dhamma* is used as meaning doctrine, law, teaching, truth —what in Theravada countries is called Buddha-Dhamma. (It can also mean, in context, righteousness, cause, and, when used in the plural, phenomena, realities, factors, conditions, moments of mental experience.)

Note that the preface to the Five Precepts contains the words, "I undertake the rule of training to refrain from...", an assertion of individual responsibility quite different from the divine *commandments* of the Hebraic and Christian decalogue.

The major dissimilarity between Buddhism and the other religions lies in the Buddhist perception of *dukkha*[2]. In Buddhism there is no more important word, no more important concept. *Dukkha* is usually translated as *suffering* but it has connotations far beyond that.

To relate what the Buddha described as dukkha serves more satisfactorily than any attempt at definition:

Birth is *dukkha*, a shocking, traumatic experience.

Sickness is *dukkha*, with its pains, its fevers, its discomforts, its anguish.

Decay, decrepitude, and old age are *dukkha*, with strength and vigor diminishing, with appetites waning, with vital organs faltering, with dependence on others increasing.

Death is *dukkha*, as is the fear of death.

Grief, lamentation, pain, anguish, and despair are *dukkha*.

Being united with what one dislikes is *dukkha*.

Being separated from what one likes or from the people one loves is *dukkha*.

Not getting what one wants is *dukkha*.

Attachment to the five *khandhas*, the five aggregates which make up an individual —body, feelings, perceptions, intentions and volitions, acts of consciousness—is *dukkha*. (More will be said about the concept of the aggregates — an

---

[2] In any discussion of Theravada Buddhism it is difficult, and inadvisable, to avoid certain Pali words, like *dukkha*, because there are simply no adequate English equivalents, but I'll try to keep them to a minimum. Anyhow, the use of Pali expressions adds flavor to discussion of the *Dhamma*.

important Buddhist concept — in subsequent pages.)
Attachment to the notion that there is a "self", a controlling, permanent, perhaps immortal unity considered to be "self" or "soul", is *dukkha*.

Impermanence, which is one of what the Buddha called the Three Characteristics of Existence, is *dukkha*.

Some Buddhist scholars, like Pra Khantipalo[3], have written that *dukkha* should not be translated as suffering because there is plenty of experience in the world which is pleasant but ,like all conditioned things, is impermanent, and therefore even though it is not suffering it is *dukkha*.

What the man born as Siddartha Gotama saw before he became the Buddha was that in the cycle of life human beings endure *dukkha*. What he set out to seek was a way for them to put an end to their *dukkha*, and it was this that he found when he became fully enlightened at the age of thirty-five and devoted the remaining forty-five years of his life to teaching. As he himself frequently put it, in a succinct summary: "What I teach is *dukkha* and the cessation of *dukkha*".

The *Dhamma* is essentially based on what the Buddha called the Four Noble Truths, the first of which is: There is *dukkha*.

Now, it is worth stressing, lest Buddhism be improperly regarded as a religion of negativism, that the Buddhist acceptance that there is *dukkha* does not deny that there is happiness and joy, achievement and fulfillment, ease and well-being— contained in the Pali word *sukkha*, the

---

[3] Pra Khantipalo is an English monk who was resident in Thailand for many years before moving to Australia in 1975 to become the abbot of a forest monastery meditation-retreat. He has written many books on Buddhism and many translations of Pali texts.

(Pra, an honorific, may also be spelled Phra.)

antithesis of *dukkha*. A Buddhist does, however, believe that all manifestations of *sukkha* are impermanent and therefore *dukkha*.

The Buddha explained that what causes *dukkha* is craving, and this, he said, is the **Second Noble Truth**. The **cessation** of *dukkha* — which leads to the attainment of *nirvana* — is achieved by the elimination of craving. This, he said, is the **Third Noble Truth**. And the attainment of *nirvana*, he said, is accomplished by following the Noble Eightfold Path, the **Fourth Noble Truth**.

The Buddha specified eight principles in his Noble Path, contained in three groupings: those principles required for the **cultivation of ethical conduct**, those required for the **cultivation of mental discipline**, and those required for the **cultivation of insight-wisdom**.

The moral and the mental cultivations are what most Western Buddhists find especially rewarding, perhaps because they are the easiest to comprehend and embrace, and it is with these that they usually begin their practice of Buddhism, their embarking on the Path.

Many however have difficulty with the insight-wisdom teachings — especially as they pertain to no-self — regarding them as being beyond their understanding. They feel that notions of no-self, no-soul, no "I" are alien to Western belief and can be understood only by the Asian mind. Actually, the teachings of insight-wisdom are not so arcane or esoteric as to be incomprehensible to the Western mind, but they do require intense effort as recommended in the Noble Path.

The cultivation of insight-wisdom is indispensable to attainment of enlightenment, which is the goal of a Buddhist, and we'll return to it after we consider the ethical-conduct and mental-cultivation disciplines.

CHAPTER TWO

THE CULTIVATION OF ETHICAL CONDUCT

I once asked an English artist why he had become a Buddhist. His answer was, "I didn't *become* a Buddhist. I realized that I *am* a Buddhist." Most Western Buddhists will agree, in that on first encountering the *Dhamma* they realized that it confirmed what they innately believed, especially the teachings about ethical conduct.

The realization, however, that one is a Buddhist may be formally confirmed by repeating three times, "To the Buddha I go for refuge; to the *Dhamma* I go for refuge; to the *Sangha* I go for refuge." (A Buddhist turns to the Triple Gem for refuge — from *dukkha*.)

For those who have access to a Buddhist temple (or monk) these words, of refuge in the Triple Gem, are spoken in the presence of a monk, and are followed by saying aloud the Five Precepts. But one can be a Buddhist without going through this or any other procedure; there are no formal inductions, no initiations, no baptism. One need simply decide, "I am a Buddhist."

The individual who decides "I am a Buddhist" is making a profound personal and social statement. That individual is saying, "I believe that I should conduct myself with benevolence, compassion, joyous sympathy, and equanimity.

I believe that these qualities are the bases of ethical conduct and that ethical conduct should be the basis of society." Without these beliefs an individual cannot follow the path, the Noble Eightfold Path, going forward to mental cultivation and to insight-wisdom.

The Buddha's specific prescriptions for the cultivation of ethical conduct — namely, **Right Action, Right Speech,** and **Right Livelihood** — derive from his conception of society based on universal love (Pali: *metta*) and compassion (Pali: *karuna*).

Right Action promotes honorable and peaceful conduct, and is based on the five precepts: abstention from destroying life, from stealing, from illicit sex, from intoxicants, from falsehoods.

In abstaining from destroying life, some Buddhists, lay and monastic, will not kill insects or eat the flesh of animals, and, indeed, there are some monks who will not even destroy plant life, will not cut down a tree or a bush, will not pull out a blade of grass, will not drink water without first having filtered it to prevent the destruction of whatever living beings might be in the water.

In abstaining from stealing, there is the explicit admonition not to take that which is not offered. This is why monks do not reach out for the food or alms presented to them but instead wait until such offerings are placed in their hands, their alms-bowls, or at their fingertips.

In abstaining from illicit sex, there are explicit pro-scriptions against adulterous sex, sex with minors, sex with those who are celibate. The Buddha also advised sexual restraint and moderation for the lay person[4] (total

---

[4] In the Buddha's time total celibacy was regarded by brahmins as proper for those in youth or in old age.

abstinence, of course, for the monk).

In abstaining from intoxicants, the precept literally says "...distilled and fermented intoxicants producing heedlessness." (I once asked the abbot of a temple in Bangkok why so many Thais, presumably good Buddhists, consumed alcohol. He said he could condone it as long as they did not become "heedless"— a most liberal interpretation of the precept, but not strictly in adherence to the teachings.)

In abstaining from false speech, the precept is intended to abjure more improprieties than lying. False Speech is the opposite of **Right Speech**.

An amplification of the precept on falsehood, **Right Speech** (which, of course, derives from right thought) promotes courteous, considerate, non-contentious conduct. It requires abstention from harsh language, from slander, from gossip, and from bearing false witness, which are evidences of False Speech.

Right Livelihood promotes life instead of destroying life. It requires abstention from earning a living in any way that harms others: slaughter of animals, trading in arms, drugs, intoxicants, poisons, or living beings (including slaves and prostitutes.)

The Buddha said: Your means of livelihood should be honorable, blameless, and innocent of harm to others.

(There are some who feel that if the Buddha were living today he might modify what he said about **Right Livelihood**, since the slaughter of animals for food, and the trading of arms for a nation's security are social necessities. Perhaps. The slaughter of animals is the destruction of life, but there are those who rationalize it as being permissible in order to provide human food needs. The trading of arms leads to the destruction of life, but some rationalize that it is permissible in the defense of a nation and its people. I leave it to the brewers, vintners, distillers, and tobacconists to rationalize their own defense.)

Right Action, Right Speech, and **Right Livelihood** lie at the core of Buddhist ethical conduct. They influence all aspects of lay behavior — personal, family, fraternal, civic and social behavior— and all aspects of monastic behavior (Chapter 21). The Buddha offered specific and detailed instructions for laypersons regarding virtually every aspect of moral behavior in everyday life (Chapter 27). Moral behavior, the Buddha taught, is the first, and indispensable step, for the layperson as well as for the monk, in following the Path. Perhaps this is why some contemporary writers understandably, but erroneously, have described Buddhism as a rational moralism rather than a religion.

CHAPTER THREE:

MENTAL CULTIVATION

The second major aspect of Buddhism that attracts many Westerners is the one which deals with mental cultivation, especially as it pertains to meditation. The significance of meditation in what the Buddha taught is underscored by his having devoted to it three of the eight principles in the Noble Path: **Right Effort, Right Mindfulness,** and **Right Concentration.**

Right Effort lies in developing our will power to change our habits of thought; and in developing the insight and intuition to perceive our states of mind. The Buddha stressed the need, if one would follow the path successfully, to make a strenuous effort. Man's difficulties derive from ignorance[5], he said, not sin, and can be confronted and overcome through techniques that can be taught — if one makes the right effort to learn. It is not easy to develop virtues, to curb passions, to overcome deluded states of mind. Effective mind cultivation takes effort, commitment and persistent meditation.

Right Mindfulness requires unremitting awareness applied to every thought, every word, every deed — in order

---

[5] "Ignorance" in Buddhist terminology means not knowing or ignoring The Four Noble Truths.

to keep one's mind in control of one's senses. As Pra Khantipalo put it in *Buddhism Explained*, the Buddha taught "in great detail what to be mindful of: the body, its movements and positions, its impermanence and decay, its patchwork nature; the feelings, pleasant, painful, and neither pleasant nor painful; the moods of the mind." (There is a form of meditation, *Vipassana*, discussed below, that specifically nurtures mindfulness.)

Right Concentration is, in short, right meditation for calming the mind and developing insight-wisdom.

There exist today, and have existed in the past, many different forms of meditation, among which are those practised by the Christian monks of the Egyptian desert, by the Jains, the Sufis, the Hindu Yogins, Catholic monastics, Transcendental Meditators, Tantric Tibetans, Zen disciples, and, what will concern us here — because of their growing appeal to contemporary Westerners — the forms of meditation practised by Theravada Buddhists.

In *Buddhism, A Way of Life and Thought*, Nancy Wilson Ross gives us these illuminating words, which serve as a helpful preface to an understanding of the practice of Buddhist meditation:

"Man (sets out) in single-hearted pursuit of satisfaction as if it actually represented a *constant*. Yet, in the Buddha's view, it was this very belief in the the attainment of lasting happiness, in conventional human terms, that was the true source of suffering [*dukkha*]. Man, by his unwillingness to accept what he interprets as life's failures to give him without stint whatever he desires, finds himself caught in an emotional trap of his own making. This trap is the product of his (belief in his) ego. It takes form from the self's insatiable appetites and delusions, its enormous blind unattainable desires, its never-satisfied craving or thirst (for which the Buddhist Pali word is *tanha*). It is *tanha* which leads the individual to place a tacit demand on life which life by its very nature cannot fulfill.

"How then can a man find peace in the midst of continuous blind striving and impermanence? There is only one way, and that way must teach the development of compassionate detachment and discernment: an ever-deepening awareness of the interdependence and relationship of the individual with the cosmos. As for a definite path to the development of such awareness, with its resultant dynamic tranquility, there is only one hope: *directed meditation or constant mindfulness.*"

The type of meditation which most Western Buddhist laypersons practise is *Samatha*, the development of calm and concentration to focus and quiet the mind. *Samatha* has been likened to a cooling of the mind (and the body), and is, in those regards, being prescribed more and more frequently in the Western world by physicians in the treatment of hypertension and other cardio-vascular disorders. (See *The Relaxation Response* by Dr. Herbert Benson of the Harvard Medical School.) Indeed, those who practice *Samatha* meditation have learned that it brings them welcome serenity in a world of frenzy. The Buddha perceived this stilling of mind, this serenity, as a means to balanced behavior.

Stilling the mind is not easily accomplished. No greater evidence of the impermanence of things, as taught by the Buddha, may be found than in the workings of the mind. Only in the most intense kinds of concentration — creative, scientific, and communicative — can the mind be focussed to remain more than a few seconds on any one given subject. Ordinarily, as Buddhists say, the mind jumps unceasingly and restlessly like a monkey in a cage. The mind, they say in another metaphor, flits hither and thither like a butterfly. As unrestrained and untamed as our dreams are, no less so is our mental stream of consciousness when we are awake. In fact, psychologists tell us that we cannot sustain a random thought sequence for more than, and frequently less than, three and a half seconds. The kinetic, electric energy of the mind, has a life of its own. The goal of *Samatha* meditation is to slow down the mental activities, to control the mental wanderings, to *ignore* sensory reactions of sight, sound, smell, taste, touch, to *ignore* the kinetics of the mind.

There are several forms of *Samatha* meditation. The Buddha recommended specific forms for specific types of personality — the greedy person, the angry person, the intelligent person, and so on — and he even taught how the different types of personality reveal themselves and can be identified (by a knowledgeable monk). But the one form of *Samatha* he recommended to all persons was the breathing-in breathing-out meditation.

This form of meditation is simple to do and simple to describe. Sit on the floor — a shallow cushion is permitted — in the half-lotus position, where the legs are spread so that the knees lie on the floor and the right foot lies sole upward on the left thigh. (The full lotus position where the left foot is also made to lie sole upward on the right thigh is probably too difficult for most Westerners to sustain.) Hold your spine erect, hands in your lap with palms upward, left hand under right, thumbs touching at their tips, eyes closed or half-closed, chin in. Make yourself comfortable in this position. (You may, also, meditate while sitting erect on a hard chair, maintaining the same upper body posture.) Concentrate on the passage of breath in and out through your nostrils, or on the rising and falling of the abdomen.

Try not to let sounds, smells, sights, touch, tastes, and

especially mental activities distract you from the one thing you're doing: observing your breathing in and breathing out. Do this for at least ten minutes, try to go twenty minutes, even longer. Do it every day, morning or evening, or both.

Now, although I've described it as simple to do, it's not simple to do effectively. The mind is not easily stilled. So, don't be impatient when your mind jumps, as it will. In the middle of an in-breath your mind will jump to a business problem, a family problem, a sensual thought, a pleasant memory, a distasteful one. You'll hear a door being slammed, an airplane overhead, a baby crying, a radio playing, a horn honking. You'll feel an itch on your scalp, a twitch in a leg muscle, a stirring in your digestive system. Just try to *ignore* these distractions and get back to your concentration on breathing in and breathing out. At first you'll find it difficult and you may be discouraged. In time, as you practise meditation, you'll be able to ignore distractions for a few seconds, even a few minutes. You will not be able to ignore them for the entire time of your meditation. But no matter. Even a brief stilling of the mind is beneficial. (Some meditators — monks, especially — do succeed in stilling the mind for long enough periods of time to enter deep states of absorption and concentration — called *jhanas* — in which there is one-pointedness of mind and there are no distractions affecting the mind, no sensations other than happiness, joy, insight.)

The Buddha said: the mind is flighty, difficult to subdue, flitting wherever it chooses. To tame the mind is good. A mind tamed can bring happiness.

For many Western meditators the beneficial effects of *Samatha* are sufficient rewards for their effort: calm, serenity, tranquility, lessening of tensions. But there are, of course, other effects which the consistent meditator ultimately perceives: the realization that the *self* is not the master of sensory perceptions or mental activities; the recognition of impermanence and constant change; in short, the *awareness* or the insight-wisdom that is the goal of the form of meditation known as *Vipassana*.

When I was first introduced to meditation at Wat Saket in Bangkok, after two weeks of practice I asked the meditation master what I was supposed to get out of it and what my goals in meditation should be. I was told, don't ask, just do. I found that answer not very helpful, and I regret, now, that I was not told that my meditations were intended to still my mind and to induce insight-wisdom. Had I been told, my meditation practice would have been more effective more quickly. But I also understand, now, that the meditation master was not being flippant or unresponsive in his "don't ask, just do". For some people — and this is what Zen masters believe — "just doing" leads to an understanding of why they are meditating. For me it did not. I mention this because many of my Western friends, like me at first, become discouraged if they "just do" without understanding why.

I might add that I have found a technique that may be helpful to start-up meditators. While on one mental level I am concentrating on "observing" my breath, on another level I am picturing my mind being cooled by a gentle flow of water. Or picturing the illumination of my brain being slowly turned down as if by a rheostat. Or picturing the flames of my mind, as on a gas range, being adjusted lower and lower, until only the pilot light still burns softly.

Many meditation teachers recommend the use of a mantra, the most popular of which among Theravadins is the *Buddho* mantra: the silent wording of *Bud-* on each in-breath, *-dho* on each out-breath. *Bud-dho...Bud-dho...Bud-dho...*

One may also practice the breathing meditation before going to sleep, while lying in bed, preferably in what is called the "lion" position, on the right side, right hand on or beside the head, left arm on top of left side.

A second method of *Samatha* cultivation is the walking meditation, very popular in the East, less so in the West. In one of its forms, the meditator walks slowly back and forth, in a natural, harmonious pace, hands held loosely in front of the body or in back, eyes lowered to a spot six feet or so in advance of one's walking, being aware simply of each footfall. In another form, one is *mindful* of each and every movement and action of walking: left foot rising, moving forward, coming down. Right foot rising, moving forward, coming down. Stopping. Turning. Moving forward again. Left foot rising ...and so on.

Notice that one does not think **my** left foot, **my** right foot, does not think I am stopping, I am turning. Thus, in addition to being a *samatha* form of meditation inducing calm, it is also a *vipassana* form inducing insight-wisdom into the nature of no-self, about which more later.

Another form of *Samatha* is that practised in Transcendental Meditation, as well as in Tibetan and other meditative practices: recitation of sacred syllables, or the chanting of mantras. One such sacred syllable is the Brahmanic *Aum* — in Buddhism *Om* — the syllable believed to be the first primordial sound. In Hindu belief the creative power in *Aum* helped bring forth the world and represents all aspects of the universe.

In the well-known Tibetan mantra *Om Mani Padme Hum*, as explained by John Blofeld in *The Tantric Mysteries of Tibet*, *Om* stands for the totality of sound, the totality of existence; *Mani* for the highest value within our own mind, "the pure void which is always to be found there when the intervening layers of murky consciousness are pierced"; *Padme*, which means lotus, for the spiritual unfolding leading to *Mani; Hum* for our potential enlightenment.

Yet another form of *Samatha* meditation recommended by Theravadin Buddhists for developing calm and concentration to focus and quiet the mind is *Kasina*. One fixes one's attention on a colored disc, and then with eyes closed recalls the image. The various forms of colored discs and backgrounds — which one constructs oneself — are earth symbols, aids to one-mindedness and tranquility. *Kasina* is, however, not a widely practised form of meditation.

Vipassana meditation[6], as contrasted with *Samatha*, is the specific mental cultivation of awareness. Whereas in *Samatha* one *ignores* sensory, mental, and physical actions and diversions, in *Vipassana* one intentionally *notices* them. One is totally mindful. It can be, on a meditation retreat, an intense and demanding exercise. For minutes, hours, even days, the meditator concentrates on noticing every action, every thought, every feeling. When eating, for example, one is aware of the fork rising, coming to the mouth, of the food in the mouth, of the food being chewed, being swallowed, of the fork moving away, of the fork being put down. And so with *everything* one does or thinks, one strives to be aware and mindful of what is happening in the most minute detail.

Some meditators practice the breathing-in breathing out meditation not only for calm (*Samatha*) but also simultaneously for insight (*Vipassana*). If a distraction arises instead of ignoring it they are mindful of it, observing the kinetics of the mind: "thinking-thinking-thinking, remembering-remembering- remembering, planning-

---

[6] Monastic forms of meditations, in addition to *Samatha* and *Vipassana* described here, are described in Part III.

planning-planning", etc.in appropriate response to the distraction. And then they return to observation of breathing until the next distraction commands their mindfulness.

The goal of *Vipassana* is the realization that the five aggregates, the *khandhas* — body, feelings, perceptions, intentions and volitions (mental formations), and acts of consciousness — are constantly taking place independently of the "self"; that there is no "self", no "I", at their controls. Such awareness frees one from the attachment to "self", because it reveals the ever- changing, impermanent nature of the aggregates, thus inducing insight-wisdom about the Three Characteristics of Existence (impermanence, no-self, *dukkha*).

Whether meditating for calm or for insight, effective meditation is difficult to accomplish. The Buddha identified five hindrances to effective meditation: the desire for sensual pleasure, ill will, lethargy-and-drowsiness, agitation-and-worry, and uncertainty. These hindrances deter many from realizing the benefits of meditation.

CHAPTER FOUR:

INSIGHT-WISDOM CULTIVATION

The whole range of Buddhist discipline and Buddhist teaching culminates in the cultivation of insight-wisdom. In the Buddha's view, as previously noted, the cultivation of ethical conduct is the first requirement in the discipline.It is the indispensable foundation on which to build the cultivation of mental tranquility and mindfulness — in other words, meditation. And meditation is the discipline from which insight-wisdom is derived.

In order to attain insight-wisdom one must have the **Right View**, the view that there are three fundamental truths, Three Characteristics of Existence. One: there is *dukkha*. Two: all conditioned things are impermanent, transitory, ever-changing. Three: there is no permanent self or soul.

An important component of **Right View** is an understanding of the Buddhist doctrine called Dependent Origination, the law of causation. In his book *Buddhism, the Light of Asia*, Kenneth Ch'en described Dependent Origination as follows:

"From ignorance as cause (pre)dispositions arise. From dispositions as cause, consciousness arises. From consciousness as cause then name and form, then six sense organs, contact, sensations, craving, grasping, becoming, birth and finally old age, grief, death, lamentation, pain and despair"...twelve links in the chain of Dependent Origination.

To help clarify this difficult concept, consider the chain in reverse order. Old age and death (and the other manifestations of *dukkha*) are linked to — derive from — birth. Birth is linked to grasping (attachment to existence). Grasping is linked to craving. Craving is linked to the sensations, which derive from the contact that is linked to the six sense organs. The sense organs are linked to the body (name and form), which is linked to consciousness, which in turn is linked to the dispositions that are derived from ignorance, from either not knowing or ignoring the Four Noble Truths.

Only by breaking the links in the chain of Dependent Origination — as a result of following the Eightfold Path diligently — can one put an end to the cycle of rebirths and attain Enlightenment.

In teaching the theory of Dependent Origination, the Buddha said it would be helpful to think of it thus: "This being, that becomes; from the arising of this, that arises. This not being, that does not become; from the ceasing of this, that ceases." Dependent Origination is then the theory of cause-and- effect applied to the Buddhist notion of the cycle of life.

In order to energize **Right View** one should cultivate **Right Thought**, which means right motivation and right attitude. This involves freeing oneself from what the Buddha called the three major defilements (or blemishes of character): greed, aversion and delusion.

By greed (Pali: *lobha*) is meant grasping and covetous-ness.

By aversion (Pali: *dosa*) is meant anger, hatred, ill will and hostility.

By delusion (Pali: *moha*) is meant ignorance of the Four Noble Truths, ignorance of the Three Characteristics of Existence, or, in short, lack of insight wisdom.

Some Western Buddhists, for reasons discussed in the previous chapter, stop short of the cultivation of insight-wisdom, restricting their practice to the cultivation of ethical conduct and the cultivation of mental development largely through *Samatha* rather than *Vipassana* meditation. Those who stop short may do so because they fear that the cultivation of insight- wisdom and the practice of *Vipassana* are too demanding to be absorbed into their practical day-to-day lives, or because they cannot cope emotionally and intellectually with the concept of no-self. Usually, such individuals do not have the benefit of access to articulate Buddhist teachers or to simplified written elucidations.

In stopping short of the cultivation of insight-wisdom they know that they cannot hope to follow the path to its goal of enlightenment but instead they consciously settle — and there's nothing wrong with their doing so — for a moral and meditative way of life. However little or however much *Dhamma* they practice, it's better than not practicing at all. (And perhaps in their next lifetimes they will proceed further along the path.)

Unfortunately, much of what has been written about Buddhist insight-wisdom, especially by Asian writers, is terribly abstract, owing in large part to the different ways in which Asians understand—much more easily than do Westerners — such Buddhist concepts as *dukkha*, suffering, of *tanha*, craving, of *anicca*, impermanence, of *anatta*, no-self, of *karma*, cause-and-effect, of rebirth, of *nirvana*. The Asian writers understand and appreciate the connotations of the Pali (or Sanskrit) terms without, often, defining them adequately for the Western reader.

Dukkha has already been reviewed.

Tanha, is somewhat similar to, and related to, *lobha*, above. It means egoistic (and sensual) desire. As the Buddha viewed it, desire for eternal existence, for perpetual youth, for constant good health, for temporal happiness, and so on, are the sources of *dukkha*, of man's anguish, suffering, and unhappiness. It may lead to doing harm to others. It may lead to inner anxieties and tensions brought on by the struggle to attain what is craved, the fear of not succeeding in the attainment, or the fear of losing what has been attained. It ensnares us. The pleasures derived from sensual desire or craving, desire for eternal existence, and desire for temporal happiness cannot, Buddhism holds, satisfy our inmost longings.

We have desires (*tanha*), Buddhism teaches, because we are attached to the notion of "self", from which we can release ourselves by conscious and strenuous effort at detachment. And detachment is a consequence of the cultivation of insight-wisdom. When we detach from *tanha*, we detach from suffering.

Anicca. In defining this Pali word in *A Popular Dictionary of Buddhism*, Christmas Humphreys writes: "Buddhism teaches that everything is subject to the law of cause and effect, is the creation of preceding causes and is in turn a cause of after- effects. There is in existence, therefore, no unchanging condition of being, but only an ever-becoming flux"...impermanence.

Although impermanence — constant flux — is an absolute characteristic of all existence, there are those who are unable to recognize or unwilling to accept its reality, and these are the people who, in their delusion, the Buddha said, create for themselves a false belief in a permanent "self". Most people, however, accept the notion of impermanence, even though they have difficulty with the notion of "no-self". Insight-wisdom helps one come to grips with both notions.

Anatta, no-self. I turn again to Kenneth Ch'en in *Buddhism, the Light of Asia* for these helpful observations: "The Buddha held that belief in a permanent self or soul is one of the most deceitful delusions ever held by man, for it gives rise to attachment, attachment to egoism, egoism to cravings for pleasure and fame, which in turn lead to suffering...He held that this false belief in a permanent self is due to an erroneous conception of a *unity* behind the elements that combine to make up an individual.

"He said that he had searched everywhere for this permanent self or soul, (this unity), but found only a conglomeration of the five *khandhas* or aggregates — material body, feelings, perceptions, predispositions (intentions and volitions, mental formations), and consciousness. At any one moment, according to him, we are but a temporary composition of the five aggregates, and as these change every moment, so does the composition. Therefore all that we are is but a continuous living entity which does not remain the same for any two consecutive moments, but which comes into being and disappears as soon as it arises.

"Why then should we attach so much importance to this transitory entity, in which there is no permanent self or soul? Once we accept this truth of the non-existence of a permanent self, when we see that what we call the self is nothing but a stream of perishing physical and psychical phenomena, then we destroy our selfish desires and self-interests, and instead of suffering from anxieties and disappointments, we will enjoy peace of mind and tranquility."

One would be wise, Buddhism teaches, not to think I am in pain, but rather there is pain; not that I am angry but rather there is anger; not that I am joyful but rather there is joy. In short, not "I am" but rather "there is". And one should realize that whatever arises, i.e. whatever "there is" — pains, feelings, sensations, thoughts, emotions — passes away. It is the law of impermanence: what arises passes away. Thus, one should realize that "I", although a useful and necessary social-communicative term, cannot be regarded as a permanent "self". It should not, cannot, be clung to.

Most Western Buddhists I know are intellectually oriented — academics, professionals, writers, artists, and the like. For them there is this paradox: although they can accept, with their minds, what the Buddha said about "no-self", it is difficult for them to accept, with their hearts, so to speak, that they have no "self" which gives them control of their intellect and, indeed, of their emotions. The Westerner, especially the intellectual,is inclined to believe that he or she is "in control" and "in charge" of his or her life.

Buddhism does not gainsay this. Although there is no self, no soul, Buddhism says, as Kenneth Ch'en further explains, "there is only a living complex of mental and physical elements [the *khandhas*] succeeding one another continuously, living on the fruits of its acts. Because of this it can control itself and can exert efforts to better itself, so that by the proper discipline it is able to attain *nirvana* or deliverance." (Or — short of *nirvana*—and in terms more immediately relevant for a practical Westerner — to teach at a university, or to write a novel, or to design a building, or to succeed at any kind of sustained effort in the arts, in science, in the professions, in business.) Yes, there is that which controls, the Buddha said: *karma*, not self.

With *karma* we come to another of the difficult and frequently misunderstood Buddhist concepts. A simple but nonetheless accurate definition is that good deeds have good effects, bad deeds have bad effects, and that the effects will be felt in this life and in the next life. To a Buddhist the bad deeds one has committed in this or in previous lives are obstacles to spiritual fulfillment, or to the attainment of enlightenment, in this life. But — this life gives one an opportunity to clean the slate, so to speak, by an accumulation of good deeds, of merit, of good *karma*.

Here is further elucidation of *karma*, as provided by Huston Smith in *The Religions of Man*:

"(1) There is [according to Buddhist belief] a thread of causation threading each life to those which have led up to it and those which will follow. That is to say, each life is in the condition it is in because of the way the lives which have led into it were lived.

"(2) In the midst of this causal sequence, man's will remains free. Though the orderliness of the world sees to it that up to a point acts will be followed by predictable consequences, these consequences never shackle man's will or determine completely what he must do. Man remains a free agent, always at liberty to do something to effect his destiny.

"(3) Though these points assume the importance of causal connections in life, none of them requires the notion of a lump of mental substance (a 'self') that is passed on from life to life. Impressions, ideas, feelings, 'streams of consciousness', 'present moments' (volitional activities, as will be further explained by Walpola Rahula, below) — these are all that we find, no underlying spiritual substrata...if there be an enduring self, subject always, never object, it cannot be found."

Other important dimensions of *karma* are explained by the scholarly Sri Lankan monk Walpola Rahula in *What the Buddha Taught*:

"The Buddha's own definition of *karma* should be remembered: 'It is volition that I call *karma*. Having willed, one acts through body, speech, and mind.' Volition is 'mental construction, mental activity. Its function is to direct the mind in the sphere of good, bad, or neutral activities.'

"It is only volitional actions — such as intention, will, determination, confidence, concentration, wisdom, energy, desire, repugnance or hate, ignorance, conceit, idea of self, etc. — that can produce karmic effects."

Walpola Rahula says further: "The theory of *karma* should not be confused with so-called 'moral justice' or 'reward and punishment'. (These ideas) arise out of the conception of a supreme being, a God, who sits in judgment, who is a law-giver and who decides what is right and wrong...The theory of *karma* is the theory of cause and effect, of action and reaction; it is a natural law, which has nothing to do with the idea of justice or reward or punishment. Every volitional action produces its effects or results. If a good action produces good effects and a bad action bad effects...this is in virtue of its own nature, its own law."

An understanding of *karma* brings with it a better appreciation of the Buddhist views on rebirth. Walpola Rahula's comments are especially helpful:

"What is difficult (to understand) is that, according to the *karma* theory, the effects of a volitional action may continue to manifest themselves even in a life after death. Here we have to explain what death is according to Buddhism.

"We have seen earlier that a being is nothing but a combination of physical and mental forces or energies. What we call death is the total non-functioning of the physical body. Do all these forces and energies stop with the non-functioning of the body? Buddhism says, no. Will, volition, desire, thirst to exist, to continue to become more and more, is a tremendous force that moves whole lives, whole existences, that even moves the whole world. This is the greatest force, the greatest energy in the world. According to Buddhism, this force does not stop with the non-functioning of the body, which is death; but it continues manifesting itself in another form, producing re-existence which is called rebirth."

One may ask, if there is rebirth, why can I not recall previous lives? The Buddhist answer is, you cannot because your powers of memory are not strong enough; and a form of Buddhist meditation dramatizes this inability to remember. It calls for the meditator to recall the activities of the previous day — every one of the activities — in reverse chronological order from the moment of retiring back to the moment of arising. Then try to recall the activities of the day before, and so on. Very difficult.

Nonetheless, you and I can recall certain events from our past, even from early childhood, but we cannot — because of its trauma — recall birth. Nor what preceded it in previous lives. There are some who claim they can, and perhaps they are right. In Tibetan Buddhism they seem quite surely to be right, as is evidenced by the rigid techniques by which future Dalai Lamas are required in childhood to recall and identify things possessed in a former life.

The Buddha said that consistent meditation could bring one a recall of former lives, and it is believed that some monks have developed the ability to recall. The Buddha could recall not only his own former lives but those of all other individuals!

(I once asked the 90-year old abbot of a Buddhist temple in Sankhampaeng, near Chiang Mai, if he had this ability. He replied that this was a question no monk was allowed by the rules of the *Sangha* to answer, because to answer yes would be boastful whereas to answer no might be untruthful. A monk may not claim any spiritual attainment, powers, or degree of enlightenment. And yet I took for an answer a twinkle in the eyes of this gentle abbot as he smiled down at me from his elevated platform.)

Not to believe in rebirth is regarded in Buddhism as a Wrong View, because it implies disbelief in *karma*, which influences the form of rebirth. (Rebirth itself is due to *tanha*, the form of rebirth to *karma*.) To disbelieve in *karma* is to deny the need to behave morally not only out of a sense of virtue but also out of the conviction that the harvest of *karma* will be reaped not only in this lifetime but also in the next ... and that it may take many lifetimes before one can attain Enlightenment. A Buddhist who has **Right View** believes in *karma* and in rebirth.

According to Buddhist belief, the karmic force of one's rebirth may manifest itself in many diverse forms — insects, animals, uncorporeal gods and tormented spirits, as well, of course, as human beings, which is the most desirable form of rebirth. For only a human being has the opportunity to cultivate one's moral conduct and mental discipline and insight-wisdom — one's *karma* — in order to put an end to the cycle of rebirth and achieve *nirvana*.

Buddhism acknowledges six realms of existence, two of them happy, four unhappy. The two happy realms are those of the gods living in the heavens, and those of human beings living on earth. The gods are somewhat akin to angels; they are less subject to *dukkha* than when they were human beings, but they have not attained *nirvana*.

The four unhappy realms are those of the Titans (*Asuras*), who have been driven out of the realms of the gods because of their quarrelsome nature; the Hungry Ghosts, who are concerned only with unsatisfied craving; the Animals, whose minds are centered on food and sex; and the Hell-Wraiths. Those who are reborn into one of these unhappy realms are individuals who in their lifetimes cultivated greed (the Hungry Ghosts), aversion (the Hell-Wraiths and *Asuras*), and delusion (the Animals).

There are those Westerners — and even Asians — who regard the various invisible realms and their inhabitants as psychological states rather than real places and real beings. There are, however, those who absolutely believe in the reality of ghosts, spirits, gods, and so on. (Many Thais do.) And there are those who say, in the agnostic sense, "Who knows? Maybe it's true." I leave it to each reader to make his or her own judgments.

The Buddha in a discourse related several examples of how *karma* affects rebirth, as follows:

If one is inclined to kill, one's next life will be of short duration.

If one is inclined to abuse other people and to make animals suffer, one will have poor health in the next life.

If one is inclined to anger, one will have a poor complexion in the next life.

If one is not generous to monks, one will be poor in the next life.

If envious... insignificant.

If obdurate and haughty... low-born.

If one does not seek the teaching of monks...stupid.

He also said that the converse is true: a long next life for one who does not kill; good health for one who does not abuse people or animals; good complexion for one who resists anger; wealth and prosperity for one who is charitable and generous; an influential life for one who is not envious; a high-born rebirth for one who is not obdurate and haughty; a life of wisdom for one who has sought the teaching of monks.

(I often have heard Thai Buddhists explain people's behavior and status on the basis of their past-lives' *karma*, such as: "Khun —, a rich and powerful man, must have done many charitable things in his previous life." " That poor woman begging in the street must have been very stingy and mean in a previous life." "My uncle has very bad stomach aches because in his previous life he hated dogs and kicked them in the stomach.")

Now we turn to *nirvana*. It is the culmination of having successfully followed the Noble Eightfold Path; of having realized the realities of *dukkha*, impermanence, and no-self; of having liberated oneself from greed, aversion and delusion; of having lived morally, meditatively, and with insight-wisdom.

One who has achieved *nirvana*, who is truly enlightened, will not be reborn, will have escaped a continuity of *dukkha*. This does definitely not mean to a Buddhist that *nirvana* is extinction (other than extinction of *tanha*, extinction of self, extinction of *dukkha*) , but rather that it is an absorption into the universal, into a manifestation of energy beyond rebirth and beyond extinction.

Edward Conze in *Buddhism: Its Essence and Development* puts it this way: "We are told (by Buddhists) that *nirvana* is permanent, stable, imperishable, immovable, ageless, deathless, unborn, and unbecome, that it is power, bliss and happiness, the secure refuge, the shelter, the place of unassailable safety; that it is the real Truth and the supreme

Reality; that it is the Good, the supreme goal and the one and only consummation of our life, the eternal, hidden and incomprehensible Peace."

Christmas Humphreys in *A Popular Dictionary of Buddhism* defines *nirvana* less abstractly: "The supreme goal of Buddhist endeavor; release from the limitations of existence."

Human beings, the Buddha perceived, are, as a result of their *karma*, at differing stages of development, of perfection, of progress on the Path to *nirvana*. Those who are least advanced, least developed, have the longest path to travel, those who are most advanced have the shortest.

Buddhism has a lovely analogy likening man in his stages of spiritual development to a lotus: the stalk rises from the mud, ascends through the water, breaks through the surface, blossoms. The Buddha believed that all individuals are capable of blossoming — of attaining *nirvana* — if not in this lifetime, then eventually. What is required of them is to follow the path diligently and patiently. So, those Westerners who have recently embarked on the path — and even Asians who have long been trying to follow the path — should not be discouraged and become impatient if their practice seems not to lead quickly and easily to enlightenment and *nirvana*. Eventually they will "blossom".

To conclude Part I here is a much-quoted verse from the *Dhammapada*, "The Path of Truth", a collection of 423 of the Buddha's most frequently quoted sayings. This verse is regarded as containing "the heart of Buddhism":

Never doing any kind of evil,
    [i.e cultivating morality]
Perfecting of profitable skill,

>   [i.e mental cultivation, or meditation]
> *Purifying one's heart as well,*
>   [i.e. cultivating insight-wisdom]
> *This is the teaching of the Buddha.*

And now we turn to the Great Teacher himself.

PART II
THE BUDDHA

CHAPTER 5

MAN AND MYTH, FACT AND FABLE

The Buddha who has been venerated for the past twenty-five hundred years was, in Buddhist belief, not the first, nor will he be the last, of the Buddhas. He is the Sakyamuni Buddha, meaning the Sage of the Sakya tribe (in which he was born), or Gotama Buddha (by his family name). Buddha is a title, not a name.

Every image of the Buddha—whether painting, frieze, or sculpture — depicts a superhuman, supramundane, god-like figure. This is in reverential tribute to the Buddha's superhuman, supramundane qualities — all-seeing, all-knowing, eternal. No attempt is ever made to represent the human being, Siddartha Gotama. There is indeed no record of what Gotama looked like, other than references (in the Commentaries) to "the perfection of his physical body". He is said to have been a human being of exceptional physical appearance — tall, golden-skinned, princely in bearing, charismatic in personality.

In tracing the long life of Siddartha Gotama from birth to enlightenment, and then from Buddhahood to death, one must rely on sources that conjoin fact with fable, legend with history, the myth with the man, the human being with the super-human being.

For primary sources one turns to the Buddha's own words as recorded in his discourses, *suttas*, to the words of his disciples, and to the Buddhist scriptures, the canon contained in the *Tripitaka*. For secondary sources one turns to ancient "biographies" written long after the Buddha's death (the first of which was written two hundred years after his death and other partial ones some five hundred years later), as well as to biographies written in the nineteenth century and the twentieth by Buddhist scholars and historians.

In studying the various sources one finds considerable differences. One says, for example, that the Buddha's mother bore her son naturally; another that the conception was immaculate; another that a white elephant entered her womb. One says that Siddartha renounced his lay life after literally having seen an old man, a sick man, a dead man and an ascetic; another says that he did not actually see them but that they are symbolic; another says that he did actually see them but that they were apparitions sent to him by the gods. And so it goes: conjunctions of presumed fact and legend.

I use the words "presumed fact" for there is much about the Buddha's life that cannot be established as certain fact. Even the date of his birth is presumed, as are so many other details.

In the Buddha's time, more than five hundred years before the Christian era, information was transmitted from person to person, from generation to generation, orally, even though some people knew how to write. Oral transcripts were considered then, as they are now, to be reliable and accurate, even more so than written ones. Transcripts of the Buddha's discourses were entrusted to monks specially trained and gifted in their ability to memorize, retain, and recite them.

Written records did not come into being until hundreds of years after the Buddha's death, when scholars wrote the story of the Buddha's life in Sanskrit, Pali, Sinhalese, Tibetan, and Chinese. As a consequence of so much and so varied oral (memorized) and written (adapted) transmissions — over so many centuries — "facts" surely became obscured and altered. Much, consequently, is presumed.

Each of the ancient recorders told the story in a way that reflected his particular religious convictions, some reflecting Buddhist Mahayana influence, others Buddhist Hinayana (Theravada), other Vajrayana (Tibetan), and still others Vedic or Hindu.

To people who, as in the case of the Hindus, believed in gods and goddesses, to the animists who believed in spirits, to the Buddhists who believed in devas and the several abodes of heaven and the realms of hell, it was only natural to impute to the Buddha supernatural and god-like qualities. Of course he could perform miracles, they believed. Certainly he could communicate with the gods, and transport himself to heaven, and contend with Mara, the Evil spirit. No question that when he was born flowers fell from the skies, the blind suddenly could see, the deaf could hear, the lame could walk. Yes, to the devout, all this is easy to accept, indeed a part of their faith.

Thus, legends and mythologies about the super-human being appeared in writings about the Buddha, inspired by reverence, awe, and adoration, just as legends and mythologies abound in the stories of all the world's great religious leaders. Even now many Buddhist writings and people refer to **Lord Buddha**, not because he is regarded as a God, but rather out of reverence for his all-knowing, all-seeing supramundane qualities.

Many facts are known about the mundane, flesh-and-blood, human being. His birth, his renunciation, his studies with Vedic *gurus*, his period of asceticism, his long period of intense meditation leading to enlightenment, his forty-five years devoted to teaching disciples, his establishment of the *Sangha*, his elucidations of the *Dhamma*, his discourses — these are among the facts that we know of the Buddha's life.

It matters not whether a precise event can be fixed to an exact date, such as his birth. What matters is that he was born. It matters not whether his death was caused by eating spoiled pig's flesh or poisonous mushrooms. He died. It matters not whether his peregrinations can be mapped. He did travel from place to place, teaching. It matters not whether the precise words of his teachings can be accurately recalled. What matters is that he taught mankind, in whatever words he may have used, how to escape the sufferings of life, how to achieve enlightenment, how to follow the Noble Eightfold Path.

In what follows I have, insofar as they may be ascertained, presented the facts of the Buddha's life. But I have also accepted, and have reproduced, the legends and mythologies. The facts speak to the mind, the legends to the heart. Together they form the glorious story of the man — and his teachings — who twenty- five centuries after his death is revered worldwide, not just in Asia, but, in ever-increasing numbers, in the western world.

CHAPTER SIX

BIRTH AND INFANCY

The birthplace of the Buddha-to-be was Kapilavastu, 130 miles north of Benares, now part of Nepal, located close to its southern-most border. With the snow-clad Himalayas looming to its north, and located amongst the rivers and streams of the fertile Ganges Lowland, Kapilavastu was the home of the Sakyas, an Aryan tribe of the Gotama clan.

The father of the Buddha-to-be was Suddhodana, the ruler, or rajah, of the Sakya tribe, described in some texts as a "king". His wealth — and it was said to be great — came from rearing cattle and cultivating rice. His family was of the military and aristocratic Kshatriya caste, as prestigious and powerful in its time as the priestly Brahmin caste.

The mother of the Buddha-to-be was the "splendid, beautiful and steadfast" Maya — known as Mahamaya, the "great" Maya — daughter of Anjana, the rajah of the neighboring tribe of Koliyans. Maya had a younger sister, Prajapati, who was also a wife of Suddhodana's.

It is said that Suddhodana and Maya tried unsuccessfully for many years to conceive a child, so that when at last Maya, in her middle age, announced that she was pregnant there was great rejoicing. Maya carried for ten months and when time for delivery approached she expressed a wish to return to her parental home in the land of Koliya for the great event.

On the way to Koliya, Maya and her courtiers found themselves in Lumbini Grove (near Rumindei, Nepal) where at that time the flowers were in full bloom and "various flocks of birds sported, singing sweetly". Intending only to rest for a while in the shade of a sala tree in the midst of the abundant surrounding beauty of the grove, Maya suddenly went into labor and gave birth to a son, while standing, in what was said to be a painless delivery. She was then carried back to her home in Kapilavastu where seven days later she died. (Legend has it that a Buddha's mother will ascend to heaven soon after giving birth.) Her sister, Suddhodana's other wife, took on the responsibility of bringing up the child.

The day of birth was the full moon day of the sixth lunar month, May-June, (a holy day celebrated in Buddhist countries as *Visakha Bucha*, the very same day on which the Buddha attained enlightenment thirty-five years after his birth and the very same day on which he died at the age of eighty.)

The year is generally regarded to have been 563 B.C., but this date is only approximate; it may have been 560 B.C., or, as some scholars believe, 543 B.C., or some time in between those dates.

These then are the bare presumed facts about the Buddha's birth, but such a prosaic rendering would scarcely be edifying to those who ascribed to the Buddha such epithets as "The Enlightened One," "The Perfect Being", "The Sakya Sage", "The Conqueror", "The Omniscient One", "The King of Righteousness", and "The Blessed One". To the devout it was inconceivable that a Buddha would enter the world so simply and prosaically. A Buddha-to-be, according to them, does not emerge in so normal a manner.

Has he not, they say, spent countless previous lifetimes in preparation for his role? Does not the Jataka book contain 550 stories about the Buddha's previous lives, in animal and human forms, prior to his birth as Gotama? In the course of those previous lives did he not develop perfection of virtues far beyond those of ordinary mortals? Did he not accumulate supreme *karma* through aeons of meritorious thought and deed? Had he not become such an all-knowing being that he could — having decided that conditions were propitious for his appearance on earth for the last time — choose where and when and how to be reborn?

So legend has it that the Buddha-to-be chose Maya to be his mother, and chose the time and place of his birth. In the legendary depiction of events the Buddha-to-be assumed the shape of a white elephant, came down from the golden mountain holding a white lotus in his trunk, circled the sleeping Maya three times, trumpeted, and entered her womb through her right side — events that had been foretold in a dream of Maya's.

Immediately after his birth, according to the myth-makers, the Buddha-to-be stood erect, took seven steps northward, walking on lotus blossoms that miraculously sprang up beneath his feet, and "with the voice of a lion" said, "I am the chief in the world. I am the best in the world, the first in the world. This is my last birth, and there is now no existence again." His father thereupon bowed in reverence.

Soon after the birth a sage and prophet named Asita came to see Suddhodana's new-born son, and what he saw were the "thirty-two marks of a great man": The baby's feet were well-set, with projecting heels, and bore on their soles wheels with a thousand spokes. He had long fingers, a soft, golden skin. He had long earlobes. Soft white down grew between his eyebrows. His testicles were withdrawn like those of an elephant. When standing, his hands reached to his knees.[7]

Asita turned to Suddhodana with tears in his eyes. Suddhodana feared that Asita was crying because he foresaw misfortune for the child. But no, Asita assured him otherwise. The child was a Buddha-to-be, destined to attain enlightenment and to preach the *Dhamma*. The reason for his tears, Asita said, was that he was old and would not live long enough to see these wonders occur.

Five days after the birth came the naming ceremony, to which many brahmins of the priestly caste were invited, among whom were eight renowned seers. The brahmin seers prophesied that the child "if he dwells in a house will become a universal monarch, but if he goes forth to a houseless life he will become a Tathagata, a fully enlightened Buddha".

The seers also told Suddhodana that in the future his son would see "The Four Passing Sights"— an old man, a sick man, a corpse, and an ascetic — and that on seeing them he would renounce his life as a householder.

Suddhodana then named his son Siddartha, "he who has accomplished all his aims". But Suddhodana was determined that his son should grow up to be a universal monarch even more exalted than the father himself, rather

---

[7] Several of these "marks" (*laksana* in Sanskrit) may be seen in statues and images of the Buddha, especially long fingers, long earlobes, long arms; a small bulge or semi-precious stone between the eyebrows, representing the soft white down "emitting rays of light that illuminate the world"; the dome-shaped turban-like protuberance under the hair, standing for enlightenment; the flame on top of the head, standing for wisdom.

than renounce his royal heritage in favor of the spiritual life. So, to make sure that Siddartha would never see "The Four Passing Sights", he resolved to keep the boy always at home, in luxurious, palatial surroundings, with amusements and diversions to keep him happily occupied.

CHAPTER SEVEN

GROWING UP

Very little — only what follows — has been recorded in the ancient or modern biographies about Siddartha Gotama's life from the time of his birth until the time of his leaving home, the Great Renunciation.

When Siddartha was about seven years old, his father took him along to observe the state ploughing ceremony, and sat him on a couch under a rose-apple tree where the boy might have a good view of the activities, comfortably shaded from the sun, and attended by his nurses. The youngster crossed his legs in the lotus position; sat with his hands, right on top of left, in his lap; and meditated for the very first time. While concentrating on breathing-in and breathing-out, he went into the first of the meditative absorptions known as *jhanas*.[8]

As he sat entranced, the sun continued its westward course in the heavens. The shadows of all the trees moved with the sun, except the shadow of the rose-apple tree under which Siddartha sat; it remained stationary, protecting the Buddha-to-be. His father, aware that he was

_____

[8] In one of his discourses the Buddha told his disciples that while sitting under the rose-apple tree he had his first "intimation of deliverance"

witnessing a miracle, reacted by paying reverence, for the second time, to his remarkable son.

Another legend relates an episode that occurred when Siddartha was sixteen. His Sakya clansmen of the warrior caste complained to his father Suddhodana that the young man was living so sheltered and luxurious a life and had so neglected the manly exercises that he would be unfit in the martial arts required of their future ruler.

Siddartha requested his father to arrange a contest of archery so that he might challenge the Sakya clansmen to compete with him. He chose a bow "requiring the strength of a thousand men" and when he drew the string the sound was "like that of thunder". He then performed twelve wonderful feats of archery, or, as another source puts its, "showed his mastery in the twelve arts" — to the great admiration and complete satisfaction of his clansmen. (In apparent contradiction to this demonstration of his great strength, there are the words of the Buddha himself, who, in one of his discourses, told a group of his disciples that as a young man he had been "delicate, extremely delicate, excessively delicate.")

Also at the age of sixteen, just after his demonstration of extraordinary martial skills, Siddartha married his first cousin, a beautiful young woman named Yasodhara, the daughter of Suppabuddha, the brother of Maya. Suppabuddha had succeeded his father as rajah of the Koliyas, and it is said in some commentaries that the martial demonstration had been arranged not so much to impress the Sakya clansmen but rather to impress Suppabuddha with Siddartha's worthiness a son-in-law.

Yasodhara is described as "majestic as a queen of heaven, constant ever, cheerful night and day, full of dignity and exceeding grace." Little, however, has been written about the married life of Siddartha and Yasodhara.

There is a thirteen-year gap in the biographies of the Buddha, until he reached the age of twenty-nine, except for a passage that occurs in one of the commentaries, saying that Suddhodana, ever mindful of the prophecies of the seers, tried to make sure that Siddartha in all those years should never venture away from home and should always be surrounded with luxuries and diversions.

In the three palaces built for him by Suddhodana — one for each of the seasons, hot,cold, and rainy — the Buddha-to-be constantly heard "the melodious music of female attendants", who played on gold-edged tambourines and danced as gracefully as nymphs. "They entertained him with soft words, tremulous calls, wanton swayings, butterfly kisses, and seductive glances." It is said that he "became a captive of these women who were well versed in the subject of sensuous enjoyment and indefatigable in sexual pleasure." But is also said — and the implication is clear — that his wife Yasodhara was his "queen."

Mythology has it that finally the gods decided the time had come to rouse him from his life of luxury and send him out of the palaces and into the world so that he might see its harsh realities. Legend has it that the female minstrels regaled him so often with stories about the beauties of the fields and forests, and the lovely sights he would see in the outside world that he finally decided to venture forth and see for himself.

CHAPTER EIGHT

THE FOUR PASSING SIGHTS

At the age of twenty-nine Siddartha Gotama ventured forth, for the first time as an adult, into the outside world.

He instructed Channa, his equerry and charioteer, to harness the chariot and— did he evade the guards set by Suddhodana or by this time had they been released?— they rode towards the nearby park, drawn by four white horses, "white as lotus petals". At the side of the road they saw a man worn out with old age. His hair was gray, his back was bent, his teeth were broken. He supported himself on a cane, and he was trembling.

Siddartha, never before having seen such a sight, asked Channa what manner of human being this might be. Channa's explanation of old age and its attendant infirmities so shocked and distressed Siddartha that he ordered Channa to turn the chariot around and return to the palace. How, he said, can I take pleasure in being in the park when I see old age and its effect on beauty and strength? How can a human being tolerate old age?

On their return Suddhodana asked Channa what had happened, and, hearing the charioteer's reply, he said that Channa was ruining his plans by having taken Siddartha into the world. He ordered dancing girls to be brought to his son, thinking that sensuous pleasures and luxuries would drive from Siddartha's mind any further thoughts of leaving the world, an eventuality which the seers had predicted would dissuade him from eventuallly becoming a king, a universal monarch.

But when Siddartha went back into the palace, he was so preoccupied with his thoughts that he was indifferent to its luxuries and diversions, and he resolved to make a second excursion.

On this occasion Siddartha saw, for the first time, a sick man, with a diseased body. When Channa explained sickness and disease to him, Siddartha again was dismayed. How can the world remain gay, he wondered, under the constant threat of disease? He ordered Channa again to return to the palace, and when he was in his chambers he thought: "Since I have learned of the danger of illness, my heart is repelled by pleasures and seems to shrink into itself."

Yet a third time Siddartha instructed Channa to prepare the chariot and take him out into the world. And this time they saw a corpse. Channa explained the meaning of death and that it is the fate of all sentient beings — another shocking revelation to Siddartha: that impending destruction awaits one and all.

This time, on his return to the palace, Siddartha was not merely indifferent to the luxuries and the sensuous allurements of the women attendant on him; he was so repelled that he withdrew into solitude.

For the fourth time Siddartha and Channa rode forth from the palace, and they saw a religious mendicant, a Brahman monk. Channa explained that this man was a recluse, that he — like many men of that time — had left the world and adopted a homeless life in order to seek salvation. The Buddha-to-be at that moment came to his momentous decision.

Some ancient biographers have written that the Four Passing Sights were apparitions by the gods in order to awaken Siddartha to his destiny; others have written that the old man, the sick man, the corpse, and the monk made themselves miraculously visible only to Siddartha and Channa. But some historians and scholars consider the story of the Four Passing Sights as being attempts by the devout, centuries after the Buddha's death, to impute supramundane happenings to mundane events, as has ever been the case when men have written about the gods they adore, the heroes they admire, and the religious figures they revere.

As the rationalists would have it, Siddartha Gotama, Buddha-to-be, may be presumed to have had a sensitive nature, a probing mind, an extraordinary intelligence. By the age of twenty-nine he must have witnessed old age, sickness, and death, despite the attempts by his father to insulate him, and he must have become so distressed by these manifestations of universal suffering that he resolved to seek the cause and the cure.

Be that as it may — whether motivated by the Four Passing Sights or motivated by his sensitivity to universal human suffering — Siddartha Gotama became a renunciate. He left his world of luxury, forgoing his inheritance and his future ascension to the rulership of the Sakyas, and parting, soon after his wife had given birth to a son, from her and the new-born child. He went forth to seek knowledge and truth.

CHAPTER NINE

THE SEARCH FOR TRUTH

Some commentaries say that Siddartha went forth the very night of his son's birth; some say it was seven days later. At any rate, it is generally agreed that on being notified of the birth, he said that the child was *rahula*, a fetter — and so the child was named *Rahula*.

It is not to be inferred that Siddartha did not love his son — or his wife — but rather that he was compelled to follow his destiny as a Buddha-to-be, and that in order to do so he was compelled to break away from all fetters, all impediments, and all attachments, and depart from home and family, as did the Brahman monks of his time, (and as all monks have always done; the monastic life **is** the homeless life.)

Indeed, on the night of his departure he went into Yasodhara's chamber, saw her sleeping with her hand on the infant's head, and although he sorely wished to raise her hand so that he might gaze on his beloved son's visage, he left without doing so, lest he wake his wife and risk being dissuaded by her from parting.

He then summoned Channa and told him to saddle Kanthaka, his favorite horse. A wonderful legend has it that as they rode forth the gods held Kanthaka's hoofs in their hands preventing them from clattering on the ground lest they arouse the palace occupants. However, Mara, the Evil One, appeared, and urged the Buddha-to-be to stop and return, promising him that if he did so Mara would guarantee him a universal kingdom. This was Mara's first attempt to dissuade the Buddha-to-be, and when it was unsuccessful Mara determined to follow Siddartha and try again and again until finally he might succeed. Mara is the symbol of the evils that beset all men: greed, lust, anger, passion, delusion, all of which the Buddha-to-be was determined to reject.

At the river Anoma, beyond the territory of the Koliyas, Siddartha dismounted, exchanged his princely clothes and ornaments for the rags of a passerby, and told Channa to return to the palace and inform his father and wife that he had gone forth into the homeless life. Channa begged to be allowed to accompany his master but at last consented to return when Siddartha told him that the members of his family would be worried about his disappearance if Channa did not tell them the facts.

In departing from Siddartha, according to another wonderful legend, the magnificent white horse Kanthaka turned to take one last look, and died of a broken heart, immediately ascending to heaven where he lived as a god.

Siddartha Gotama then cut off his hair, and the shorn locks did not fall to earth but rather rose to the heavens where they were happily received by the gods, who took this miracle as a sign that they had been right in recognizing Siddartha as a Buddha-to-be.

He next went — as he told the story in one of his discourses — to Alara Kalama, a renowned Brahman monk and teacher who resided at Rajaghaya, present-day Rajgir, to seek instruction and spiritual guidance. Alara's doctrine, the Buddha said, did not conduce to "aversion, absence of

passion, cessation, tranquility, higher knowledge, *nirvana*."
Alara's teachings were based on the belief in an *atman*, an
eternal soul without which there could be no salvation. This
did not appear to the Buddha-to-be to be the truth, so he
left Alara and turned to another renowned Brahman monk,
Udraka[9] Ramaputra.

Udraka expounded on the effects of *karma* and the
transmigration of souls, and although Siddartha believed in
the doctrine of *karma* he questioned the existence of an
eternal soul and its transmigration. Nonetheless, through
his studies with Udraka, as well as with Alara, he absorbed
considerable knowledge of Brahman-Vedic beliefs, some of
which he retained in his own later teachings. He felt that
even though they had taught him everything they knew
and believed, they had left many of his questions
unanswered — especially his questions about suffering,
how it came about and how it could be eliminated.

And so he decided to continue his search for truth
elsewhere.

In the jungles of Uruvela, near present-day Bodhgaya,
he came across five ascetics who were "keeping their senses
in check, subduing their passions, and practicing austere
penance."

For the next six years, in the company of the five
ascetics, "he applied himself to mortification (and
underwent) the most severe penances." He ate so little that
his body wasted away, and when he put his hand on his

---

[9] The spellings of Udraka's name, and Alara's, and, indeed, many
of the names I have used, vary from biography to biography; for
example, Gautama sometimes appears rather than Gotama. I have
selected spellings most frequently found.

abdomen he could feel his spine. He practiced holding his breath until he almost suffocated. He tried in every way to break the hold that his body held over him. (The gaunt Buddha-to-be is depicted in statues showing him near death as result of his austerities.)

One day after he had bathed himself in the river he was so weak that he could barely rise from the water. He reached an overhead branch, pulled himself to his feet and staggered to the river-bank. There, under a banyan-tree, he swooned, fell to the ground and was close to death. His mother descended from heaven to comfort him, and he promised her that he would not die but would live to become a Buddha.

Siddartha had learned that austere asceticism was not the path to truth, but rather to death, which would have put a premature end to his striving for enlightenment. Therefore he determined to begin nourishing his body again, and when he announced his decision, the five ascetics renounced him and abandoned him.

Now, it happened that this very banyan-tree under which the Buddha-to-be had swooned was the one to which a girl named Sujata had previously prayed that she might have a son. When her baby was born it was indeed a son, and Sujata sent her maid Punna to prepare the ground at the foot of the banyan-tree for an offering of thanks. Punna saw Siddartha sitting against the tree and thought he must be the spirit of the tree come down to earth. When she reported this to her mistress, Sujata prepared a meal of special rice-milk and offered it to Siddartha in a golden bowl. As she withdrew she said, "May you achieve the goal to which you aspire."

Siddartha ate the rice-milk beside the river-bank and then, because he had had a dream that he was on the verge of becoming a Buddha, he placed the bowl in the stream of the river, thinking: if this bowl should float upstream rather than down, it will be a sign that the dream was true, and that I shall become a Buddha.

The bowl moved to the middle of the stream and then, despite the strong downstream current, it floated upstream. The sign had been given.

CHAPTER TEN

THE TRUTH DISCOVERED

Revived by Sujata's rice-milk, Siddartha recalled the meditation he had experienced when he was seven years old, and the *jhana* it had induced, and he decided that he would now sit and meditate intensely, concentrating uninterruptedly on the nature of life, the nature of reality, the nature of self, and especially on the nature of suffering, its cause, and its elimination. He walked to the nearby town of Gaya (Bodhgaya) and sat under a bodhi-tree *(ficus religiosa)*, what came to be known as "the tree of wisdom".

How long he meditated under the bodhi-tree is not truly known. Some commentaries say seven days, some say as many as forty-nine days, and some say he attained enlightenment on the very first night. However long his meditation might have lasted he arose at last as the Buddha, fully enlightened!

So grand an event later inspired wonderful legends. One legend concerns Muchalinda, the king of the *nagas*. These were creatures somewhat in the shape of a sea serpent or perhaps of a dragon. Their heads were hooded, like those of the giant cobras. One day, in the midst of a storm, the *naga* king came to the future Buddha, arranged its great coils to form a seat for him, and raised its hood over his head to protect him. (The *naga* has ever since been revered in Buddhist legend, and *naga* forms may be seen in many Buddhist temples, as well as in paintings and statuary.)

The most famous legend concerns the reappearance of Mara, the Evil One, who came to the future Buddha as he sat under the bodhi-tree, and summoned all his powers to prevent Siddartha Gotama from attaining enlightenment. If Gotama were to do so he would prevail over evil and thus destroy Mara's realm. So, Mara directed against Gotama the forces of whirlwind, storm, hot rocks, burning coals, sands and mud, but as they approached Gotama these forces lost their strength and subsided harmlessly.

Next, Mara summoned other forces to attack Gotama with spears, arrows, clubs, and other weapons, but not only did they fall harmlessly at Gotama's feet, they turned miraculously into fragrant flowers.

Mara then turned to his daughters, Desire, Discontent, and Passion, and they along with hordes of dancing girls attempted to divert Gotama. In vain.

And then, touching a finger to the ground before him, Gotama asked the earth to bear witness to his rightful struggle for enlightenment. The earth responded with a frightful roar, and the earth goddess twisted from her coiled hair a flood of water that swept away all of Mara's forces, whereupon Mara withdrew in defeat.

There are many versions of the future Buddha's struggles with Mara, and they are be taken symbolically, as representing Gotama's struggles to overcome his fetters and defilements, the same fetters and defilements that make it so difficult for human beings to attain enlightenment.

In the "fourth watch" of the night, as dawn was breaking — it happened on the day of the full moon of *Visakha*, the same day as his birth — Gotama attained full enlightenment, he reached the state of supreme knowledge, he achieved Buddhahood. The earth swayed as if dancing, the gods appeared in the heavens to witness the event, thunder boomed loudly above, flowers and lotus blossoms fell from the sky to carpet the ground around the Buddha.

The Buddha later said, in a discourse, that there arose in him at the moment of enlightenment the knowledge of his emancipation, the realization that the cycle of rebirth was ended for him. Ignorance was dispelled, he said, and knowledge arose. Darkness was dispelled, and light arose. And in that same discourse he said enlightenment comes similarly to those who are vigilant, strenuous and resolute in their practice of the *Dhamma*.

Mara then made one last effort. He said to the Buddha, it is pointless to expose the *Dhamma* to mankind, since its truth is too profound for any human being to understand. The Buddha, he argued, had achieved *nirvana*, so why not accept it and withdraw into it? The Buddha answered, " There are some who will understand", and Mara went away, not to appear again until forty-five years later, three months before the Buddha's death.

By this legend we are meant to understand that the Buddha did, indeed, at this critical moment in his life, wrestle with his conscience. He had after all attained full enlightenment; he had eliminated, for himself, *dukkha*; he would never again be subject to *samsara*, the endless, fruitless carousel of birth, death and rebirth. Why bother trying to preach to mankind the truths that he had discovered? Why subject himself to what might be frustration and disappointment in doing so?

But no, those arguments could certainly not prevail. He was a Buddha, he would not turn his back on the sufferings and sorrows unenlightened mankind endlessly endured.

CHAPTER ELEVEN

REVEALING THE TRUTH

The Buddha now set off to find his old teachers, Alara and Udraka, to share his new-found knowledge with them, but learning that they had died, he headed for Benares where the five ascetics who had recently abandoned him had gone to live.

On the way he met a former acquaintance, a Jain monk named Upaka, who was struck by the majestic appearance of the Buddha, by the "pure and clean" color of his skin. Upaka asked him to name the master under whose guidance he had renounced the world. The Buddha replied that he had no master, that no man was equal to him, that "alone I am the All-Enlightened, I have won coolness, won *Nirvana*."

Upaka asked where he was going, and the Buddha told him, to Benares "to give light to those enshrouded in darkness". Skeptical, Upaka said, "Would that it might be so. Your way lies yonder." Then he shook his head, turned away and went in the opposite direction. So, the first man to have met the Buddha rebuffed him.

At the Deer Park of Isipatana (now called Dhamek) three miles north of Benares, the Buddha came across the five ascetics who had been his former companions. What happened next was narrated by the Buddha in one of his discourses. The five ascetics, believing that Siddartha Gotama had abandoned a life of austerity for one of abundance, also rebuffed him. They agreed among themselves not to greet him and not to rise in respect, but they would allow him, if he so wished, to sit down.

Somehow, however, one of the ascetics, Kondanya, perceived that there was something special about this man they had known as Siddartha Gotama, and addressed him by name and as "friend". The Buddha replied that this form of address was now improper, that he was an *arahant*, a fully enlightened one, that a Buddha brought salvation to the world and should be treated with the same respect that children show their fathers.

He convinced the ascetics that he had not turned to a life of abundance. He told them that in his recent enlightenment he had learned how to eliminate suffering and sorrow, that he had learned how to attain the supreme peace, and that he could instruct them how to do so. Whereupon the Buddha delivered his first discourse, known as The Turning of the Wheel of the Law, a Pali phrase which literally means: To set rolling the royal chariot-wheel of a universal empire of truth and righteousness.

(A special Wheel is frequently pictured in Buddhist art as a symbol of the *Dhamma*.) In this first discourse[10] the Buddha set forth the fundamental principles of the Truth as it had been revealed to him in his enlightenment. His words were a very summation of the *Dhamma*.

---

[10] The first sermon is commemorated by all Buddhists on the holy day of *Asalha Bucha*, the day of the full moon of the eighth lunar month, so it is assumed that the Buddha delivered this historic, world-changing sermon to the ascetics two lunar months after his Enlightenment.

Here is what the Buddha said, in paraphrase:

Two extremes are to be avoided: the extreme of indulgence in sensuality and worldy pleasures and the extreme of austerity, mortification and self-torture. Austerities produce confusion and sickly thoughts, while sensuality is enervating and makes man a slave of his passions. One should follow the Middle Path which keeps aloof from both extremes. One should satisfy the necessities of life. One should keep one's body in good health and one's mind strong and clear in order to comprehend the Four Noble Truths.

The First Noble Truth is the existence of suffering (*dukkha*). Birth is suffering, old age is suffering, sickness is suffering, death is suffering. Sorrow, lamentation, dejection and despair are suffering. Contact with unpleasant things is suffering; not getting what one wishes is suffering. States of mind that co-exist with a consciousness of self are states of suffering.

Suffering must be comprehended and its cause given up.

The Second Noble Truth is that the cause of suffering is craving (*tanha*), craving for rebirth, accompanied by delight and greed, craving for pleasure and sensuous experience, craving for existence, craving for non-existence.

The Third Noble Truth is the cessation of suffering, the liberation from it. (*nirvana*)

The Fourth Noble Truth is that the path leading to cessation of suffering is the Noble Eightfold Path, which consists of Right Views, Right Intention, Right Speech, Right Action, Right Livelihood, Right Effort, Right Mindfulness, and Right Concentration.

(The various aspects of the Noble Eightfold Path are grouped under three headings: Morality, Meditation, and

Insight Wisdom —as explained in Part One.)

These truths, he told the five ascetics, he had learned while meditating under the bodhi-tree. They were the truths that led to his enlightenment, and whose comprehension could help any human being attain enlightenment.

Thus, in his First Sermon, the Buddha taught the five ascetics the fundamentals of what was to become one of the world's great religions, or, as some would have have it, one of the world's great philosophies —a way of life, a path toward individual salvation, a path that is today followed by an estimated 310 million men and women.

The first of those millions were the five ascetics themselves who, after hearing the Buddha's wisdom, asked to be accepted as his disciples and became the first members of the *Sangha*, the Buddhist monastic order. Their names were: Kondanya, Vappasana, Bhaddiya, Mahanama, and Assaji.

The Buddha then, in his second sermon, taught his first monastic disciples the doctrine of non-self, that all existence is transitory or impermanent, that the concept of a permanent self is a delusion. The belief in a permanent self (or soul), he told them, leads to attachment to egoism, which in turn leads to craving for pleasure and sensual satisfaction, which in turn leads to suffering. What we regard as self is merely a conglomeration of the five aggregates (*khandhas*) — material body, feelings, perceptions, predispositions (volitions), and consciousness — each of which is constantly changing, arising and disappearing.

During the next three months the Buddha remained in the Deer Park at Benares, and as word of him and his teachings spread, men and women, kings and commoners, "high and low, ignorant and learned", came to listen to his discourses, and to become his disciples.

The first to do so, after the five ascetics, was a rich young man from Benares named Yasa. Like the Buddha himself, Yasa had become disenchanted with his life of luxury and sensuality, and came to the Buddha for guidance. After hearing the Buddha explain the Doctrine, Yasa is said to have attained enlightenment. His example inspired fifty-four male friends of his to come to the Buddha, embrace the *Dhamma*, and join the *Sangha*. In addition, Yasa's mother and former wife became lay disciples, the first lay women to do so.

Now the number of monks in the *Sangha* had grown to sixty, and these sixty the Buddha dispatched "in different directions", telling them, "Go forth, monks, and teach the truth, which is glorious in the beginning, the middle, and the end, for the good of all beings. There are some whose eyes are not obscured by dust. Teach them, they will understand."

With the Going Forth of the Sixty the seeds were sown for the subsequent growth and spread of Buddhism beyond the areas of northern and eastern India — in the first centuries into all the countries of Asia and in later centuries into the West.

Note that the Buddha instructed his monks to "teach". The use of the word, teach, is significant. Neither the Buddha nor his disciples attempted directly to proselytize, nor have Buddhists ever done so, for a Buddhist respects all religions. The spread of Buddhism for more than twenty-five hundred years has occurred because people have recognized in the Buddha's teachings a truth intensely and personally meaningful to them, a path to enlightenment.

CHAPTER TWELVE

TEACHING THE TRUTH

Having revealed to those who became his first disciples the fundamentals of the Truth — the Doctrine, the *Dhamma* — and having found that there were indeed those who would understand, who were receptive and grateful, the Buddha now set out to teach any and all who sought his instruction.

In Uruvela the Buddha delivered his third sermon, the famed Fire Sermon. The circumstances, part legend and part historical, were as follows:

Three brothers who resided at Uruvela were fire-worshipping acsetics named Kasyapa who had attracted a large following of adherents. The Buddha — according to legend — performed many miracles for the Kasyapas and their one-thousand followers. He overcame two *nagas* who spewed smoke and flame. He called forth a great flood and then rescued the fire-worshippers from it. He created stoves in which they could heat water for their bathing. And try as they might the Kasyapas were unable to light fire, prevented from doing so by the Buddha's magic powers. In these ways the Buddha, it was believed, had shown his aversion to the practice of fire-worship.

After performing the miracles the Buddha delivered his discourse. As long as men remained in ignorance, he said, they would behave as if consumed by fire: the fire of passion, the fire of hatred, the fire of attachment and delusion. Men are on fire, he said, with birth, old age, death, sorrow, lamentation, misery, grief and despair. Fire acted on men through their six senses, eyes, ears, tongue, nose, body, and mind (mind being according to Buddha the sixth sense) — whose stimuli are the manifestations of what they perceived to be "self" — and those who learned how to control their reactions to sense stimuli could, in effect, extinguish the fire, thus putting themselves on the path to enlightenment.

After hearing this discourse and perceiving its truth, the one thousand listeners, including the Kasyapa brothers, asked the Buddha to accept them as his monastic disciples.

Accompanied by his new disciples, the Buddha then proceeded to Rajaghaya. The powerful King Bimbisara and a multitude of his subjects, came to visit, out of curiosity as to whether this now- heralded man was the pupil of the better-known oldest Kasyapa brother, or vice versa. Kasyapa bowed at the feet of the Buddha, and said, "He is my teacher, I am his disciple."

The Buddha then delivered a discourse, and Bimbisara, out of gratitude for having been instructed, made the Buddha a gift of a bamboo grove, Veluvana, where he and his monks were invited to remain for the rainy season (and where the Buddha resided for many rainy seasons thereafter.)

Two renowned ascetics of Rajaghaya, Sariputta and Moggallana, came to the Buddha in the bamboo grove and, recognizing him as the great teacher, asked to be accepted as disciples. Within a week Moggallana attained enlightenment — a quick and remarkable culmination of his monastic practice — and within two weeks Sariputta. The

Buddha then appointed them to be leaders of the *Sangha*.

(It is presumed that enlightenment came to Sariputta and Moggallana so quickly — as it did to others who received instruction directly from the Buddha — as a result not only of the Buddha's potent influence, but also of the "perfections" they had developed in previous lives. The Buddha himself said that not all people are ready to attain enlightenment; their imperfections, a consequence of their *karma*, are such that it may take them many, many lifetimes of intensive devotion to the path of purification.)

A most significant act of the Buddha's soon thereafter, the *Sangha* having grown so impressively, was to establish the *Vinaya*, the rules of discipline for the monastic order, which included the monastic precepts known as the *Patimokkha*.[11] However many precepts the *Patimokkha* contained at its first promulgation is not known for certain, but when it came to be recorded in written form, it contained two hundred twenty-seven, covering every aspect of monastic behavior (Chapter 21).

Around this time it became evident that enthusiasm for the Buddha and his teachings was not universal. There were those who resented his popularity and his having converted so many to his beliefs. They accused the Buddha of being responsible for the break-up of families, for the "creation of widows", for encouraging childlessness. They abused and ridiculed the monks on their alms-rounds.

The Buddha advised his monks not to engage in dispute with their antagonists but simply to tell them that the

---

[11] The occasion of the Buddha's recitation of the Patimokkha to his 1,250 *Arahants*, is commemorated by Buddhists on the day of the full moon of the third lunar month. This holy day is known as *Makha Bucha*.

Buddha was only trying to spread righteousness, that neither he nor they proselytized directly but that the Buddha won converts only by proclaiming the truth — which he did for the benefit of all. The antagonism thereupon subsided within seven days.

CHAPTER THIRTEEN

REUNION WITH HIS FAMILY

When the Buddha's father, Suddhodana, became aware of his son's fame he sent couriers to ask him to return home for a visit. The Buddha did as his father requested, and his return occasioned many wondrous events.

One of his first acts on his return was to deliver a discourse to his father and his father's court. His words won the favor of those who were able to hear them, but the townspeople outside the palace remained skeptical and indifferent, too proud to pay reverence to the former Siddartha Gotama. The Buddha then, legend has it, levitated several feet above the ground and performed the "Miracle of the Pairs". He made flames emerge from his upper body and streams of water from his lower. Then he made the flames emerge from his lower body and the streams of water from his upper. Then he created several variations of flames and water. None who witnessed the miracles could remain skeptical. For the third time the Buddha's father paid him reverence, as did the townspeople.

The next morning the Buddha and the monks who had accompanied him went out with their bowls on their customary alms-round to walk from house to house so that they might be offered food. When he was informed about this, Suddhodana rushed out to his son and asked, "Why do you go begging? Why do you put us to shame? Surely, I can provide food for you and your monks so that you need not go from house to house, bowls in hand."

The Buddha replied, "It is our custom."

His father rejoined, "It is not the custom of those of royal lineage."

The Buddha said, "Your lineage may be royal, father, but mine is the lineage of Buddhas, and this is our custom."

Suddhodana stood aside but then led the Buddha to the palace where the whole family, except Yasodhara, his former wife and the mother of his son Rahula, gathered to pay him honor. Yasodhara remained in her quarters, saying, "If he values me, he will come to me."

The Buddha did go to her, and she, even though she knew that she should not embrace a member of the *Sangha* or touch any part of his body, could not refrain from prostrating herself before him, in awe and respect, putting her arms around his feet.

The next day another wondrous event occurred. The Buddha's half-brother, Nanda, came to the Buddha, and even though this was the very day on which he was to be married, asked to be ordained. The Buddha asked him if he truly desired to leave the world, and Nanda, out of great reverence for his half-brother as well as having been inspired by the Buddha's sermon, avowed that he did. The Buddha thus accepted him for ordination into the *Sangha* so that he might follow the path.

A few days later Yasodhara sent Rahula to visit the Buddha and ask for his inheritance, telling him that his father had once been a man of great wealth. When Rahula saw his father he was overcome with love and admiration, but nonetheless asked the "golden-colored ascetic" to give him his inheritance. The Buddha reflected: "Wealth perishes in the using and causes nothing but vexation", and decided that far better it would be to give him the "noble wealth" that he had acquired under the bodhi-tree, and make him the heir of a "spiritual inheritance". The Buddha then asked his aide Sariputta to ordain the boy Rahula as a novice, it being a requirement for full ordination as a monk that a man be twenty years of age.

Suddhodana was distressed at having lost his son Nanda and his grandson Rahula to the *Sangha*. He came to the Buddha, yet another son whom he had lost, and made a request that was to have lasting significance. He asked the Buddha to establish a ruling that no one in the future be accepted for ordination without the permission of his parents. The Buddha agreed, and the rule has pertained from that day to now (and includes the provision that a married man must have the permission of his wife.)

Subsequently the Buddha left Kapilavastu and headed back to Rajaghaya. On the way he encountered two cousins, Ananda and Dewadatta, who were in the company of two friends, Upali and Anuruddha. This was a most momentous encounter, for these four men, who asked to be admitted into the *Sangha*, were later to play very important roles.

Ananda was to become the Buddha's closest attendant. Dewadatta was to become the Buddha's rival and the leader of an intended schism. Upali, who had been a barber, a man of low caste, was to become a leader in the *Sangha*, evidence of the Buddha's disregard of a man's humble origins or caste. And Anuruddha was to become a great interpreter of the Buddha's teachings.

When the Buddha returned to Rajaghaya a householder of nearby Savatthi named Sudatta, and known as Anathapindika, "giver of alms to the unprotected", was so favorably impressed by the Buddha that he invited him to spend the rains retreat at Savatthi. The Buddha accepted, and Anathapindika found an ideal spot, a grove owned by Prince Jeta, but was told by Jeta that he would not sell the grove even if Anathapindika were to cover it with millions of gold pieces.

When the devout Anathapindika proceeded to do exactly that and had managed, through his own efforts and those of other devout followers, to cover all but a small part of the grove with gold pieces, Prince Jeta decided not only to sell the grove but to donate the uncovered part as his gift to the *Sangha*. Thus was founded the monastery of Jetavana.

A wealthy laywoman named Visakha went to the Jetavana monastery to hear the Buddha preach. She was wearing a very costly bejeweled headdress, which she took off and set aside before entering the monastery. Ananda put the headdress in a safe place while Visakha went inside to listen to the Buddha's discourse. When she emerged she decided to devote an amount of money equal to the value of the headdress for the construction of a monastery for the Buddha and his monks in the Pubabarama, the Eastern Park.

CHAPTER FOURTEEN

WHY HIS TRUTH WAS ACCEPTED BY SO MANY

How did it come about that the Buddha was able to attract so many monastic and lay followers, and to inspire such generosity from people like Anathapindika and Visakha?

One reason, according to a distinguished American professor[12] of comparative religion, is that the religion preached by the Buddha was unique and in many regards quite different from what the Indians were accustomed to. It was devoid of authority; "Be ye lamps unto yourselves". It was devoid of ritual; the Buddha regarded ritual as a fetter. It was devoid of speculation; the Buddha refused to discuss metaphysics. It was devoid of tradition; "Do not ye go by what is handed down, nor on the authority of your traditional teachings". And it was devoid of the supernatural; the Buddha — legends to the contrary — deplored divination, forecasting, and soothsaying, which he thought speciously diverted people from the principles of the Noble Eightfold Path.

Another reason is that what the Buddha preached was *dukkha* (which affects all beings) and its elimination (which

---

[12] Huston Smith, *The Religions of Man*, Harper & Row Publishers.

all desire). However, to make men aware of the meanings and ramifications of *dukkha*, as well as its elimination, the Buddha had to teach them many things, he had to expound the many facets of the *Dhamma*.

In teaching the *Dhamma*, the Buddha taught men the Four Noble Truths and the Eightfold Path.

He explained to them that the concept of "self" is an illusion.

He taught them that all things are impermanent.

He told them that the great impediments, the fetters, to enlightenment are greed, anger and delusion.

He further told them that one combats greed with generosity and renunciation, aversion with loving-kindness and compassion, delusion with wisdom.

He explained the concept of *karma*, that good acts induce good consequences, evil acts evil ones.

He further explained the concept of rebirth, in which one's karmic energy prevails through many lifetimes influencing one's future rebirths and future lives.

He urged them to avoid "attachment".

He taught them the fundamentals of moral behavior.

He showed them how to meditate in order to induce tranquility and insight wisdom.

He advised them not to take excessive delight in their good fortune nor excessive despair in their bad fortune — because neither was permanent or enduring.

He told them not to regret the past nor fret about the future.

He showed them how to attain enlightenment.

It was not only through the manifest truth of his teachings but also through his remarkable presence and personality that the Buddha was able to convey his message so effectively. He could communicate easily with the elite

— the kings and potentates — for he himself was of the elite class. He could communicate comfortably with commoners, adapting his language to the ability of his audiences to comprehend it. He was compassionate towards all, never losing patience, ever striving to be helpful, to be sympathetic, to teach and to enlighten.

To be in the Buddha's presence was to be transformed, so great was the force of his spiritual aura. With few exceptions, all who came into his presence experienced a sense of awe, adoration, and reverence. He was regarded by many as if he were divine, but he rejected such description, saying that he was neither a god, nor a saint, nor an angel, but rather a human being, an **awake** human being.

The religion taught by the Buddha was empirical. Your level of understanding, your personal experience, he said, is the ultimate test of the truth. Don't merely take what I or others tell you on faith. Don't believe blindly. Find out for yourself by following the path.

His approach was centered in the individual, in that he said, don't look to a divinity for your salvation. Look only to yourself.

His advice was practical. He urged his disciples not to speculate on matters of cosmology or theology, but to devote their efforts to finding solutions within their capability, using the *Dhamma* as their tool.

The *Sangha* he founded was democratic, open to all, be they of high caste or low or even "untouchables", be they rich or poor, be they nobles or peasants. Whether his followers were to become monks or to remain laypersons, he welcomed them, taught them, inspired them, and set them on the path to enlightenment.

The *Sutta Pitaka*, one of the three sections of the *Tripitaka*

— the complete Theravada Buddhist scriptures — is the Volume of Discourses, consisting of the discourses, the sermons, delivered by the Buddha and by his Noble Disciples. There are in this Volume 17,500 (!) discourses — which explain and illuminate the *Dhamma*, the Truth as seen by the Buddha.

In the forty-five years from his enlightenment to his *Parinirvana* there was hardly a day in which the Buddha did not devote himself to teaching. Teaching the *Dhamma* was his mission and he completely devoted his life to it, delivering to monks and to laypersons discourses that were relevant and germane to each audience.

In addition to his sermons and discourses the Buddha spent time each day in private sessions with monks or laypersons who wanted his individual counseling, his comforting, or merely his companionship.

But — three times a day he withdrew in order to meditate in seclusion. Thus, by his actions as well as his words, he inspired his disciples to follow the path.

CHAPTER FIFTEEN

LATER YEARS

No accurate chronology has been recorded for most of the years of the Buddha's life, but several major episodes, legendary and factual, some dated and some not, are narrated in various discourses, commentaries, and biographies.

When the Buddha was forty years old, and was living in the Mahavana grove near Wesali, he learned that his father Suddhodana was dying. Accompanied by Nanda and Rahula, he "flew through the air" to his father's bedside, comforted him with words of *Dhamma*, sat with him as he attained *nirvana*, and ceremoniously conducted the cremation of his body.

At about this time the Sakyas, over whom Suddhodana had ruled, and the Koliyas, whose ruler Suppabuddha was the father of the Buddha's wife Yasodhara, were engaged in bitter quarrels over irrigation rights on the river that marked the border between their lands. The outbreak of armed conflict was averted only through the Buddha's eloquent intercession. He preached to both sides. He told them that the blood of their kinsmen was more precious than the water from the river and should not be risked by warfare. He persuaded them to seek an agreeable compromise and he brought about their reconciliation.

Suddodhana's widow Prajapati and the aunt of the Buddha, who had become his foster mother after his mother's premature death, now came to him and requested permission to be ordained as a nun (*bhikkuni*). The Buddha said no, women could not be ordained. Three times Prajapati made her request, and three times the Buddha said no.

There were three reasons behind his refusal. One, women had their household and societal duties to perform, keeping the family together, and bearing and rearing children. Two, it would be too arduous for a woman to rise before dawn, to walk for food with an alms-bowl, to eat whatever might be placed in it, and to follow the other austerities required of monastic life. Three, since one of the inviolable precepts of monks was chastity, the violation of which resulted in expulsion from the *Sangha*, it would be unwise to permit women to co-exist with monks in a monastery.

Prajapati persisted. She followed the Buddha to the Mahavana grove, accompanied by other Sakya women, cut off her hair, donned yellow robes, and again appeared before the Buddha to seek his permission, thrice. Again the Buddha refused, thrice. But Ananda interceded on Prajapati's behalf, and asked the Buddha if he felt that a woman was not capable of attaining enlightenment, arahantship, *nirvana*. The Buddha answered, Ananda, of course a woman is capable. Ananda said, if that then is the case, should not women be allowed to enter the *Sangha* and follow the path? And the Buddha at length said, yes, he would so allow, but only if they would agree to eight very strict rules which regulated their behavior toward monks.

Prajapati agreed to the eight rules and was ordained, thus becoming the first Buddhist nun. But the Buddha appears to have regretted his consent to the ordination of women, for he told Ananda that were they not to have been ordained, the doctrine of Buddhism would last one thousand years. Now, however, it would last only five hundred. (Centuries later, having recognized that the doctrine had already lasted five hundred years, revisionist historians wrote that the Buddha said "ten thousand" and "five thousand" years, rather than "one thousand" and "five hundred".)

The Buddha's wife Yasodhara entered the Order at the same time as Prajapati. In a short time seventy women were accepted as nuns —and later four hundred thirty more. The best-known among them were King Bimbisara's wife Khema and a woman named Kisa Gotami, who appears in the scriptures in the Parable of the Mustard Seed (narrated in Chapter Sixteen).

As a preface to the story about the Buddha's visit to his mother in heaven: Buddhism acknowledges that human beings with exceptionally good *karma* can be reborn as *devas* to live in one of the heavens, but that they have not yet attained the state of *nirvana* in which there will be no future rebirths. They are still victims of *dukkha* and impermanence (*anicca*), committed to the wheel of life, (*samsara*) — death and rebirth, death and rebirth.

In the seventh year of his ministry the Buddha went to visit his mother in one of the heavens[13] where she had ascended at her death seven days after his birth and was residing as a deva with the mothers of previous Buddhas and with other gods. He stayed with her during the three-month rains season, preaching the *Dhamma* to her and the

---

[13] The heaven of the thirty-three gods, Tavatimsa (Pali)

other assembled *devas*. When his mother and the *devas* had been fully instructed in the attainment of *nirvana* the Buddha returned to earth, descending on a bejewelled staircase, and was greeted by a multitude of his disciples. (This event, along with all the other legendary events, is frequently depicted in beautiful friezes, paintings, and temple murals.)

Soon after the visit to his mother the Buddha encountered a series of serious problems.

It was not long after his descent from heaven that a young woman named Chinca was persuaded by members of an antagonistic ascetic Order to defame and discredit the Buddha. She set out to do so in a very sly manner.

The Buddha was at that time residing at the Jetavana monastery, and people of the nearby town would come to the monastery in the morning to spend the day there and to listen to the Buddha's sermons. Chinca would dress herself in colorful garments, bathe her body with perfumes, and, pretending that she had spent the night at the monastery, would appear in the morning as the townspeople were approaching. This she did so often that the townspeople began to question her. Her deceitful reply was that she had spent those nights in the monastery alone in the chambers of the Buddha.

After a few months of this terrible deceit, Chinca went even further in her attempt to defame the Buddha. She donned excess clothing to make her appear pregnant, and one day approached the Buddha while he was preaching, and interrupted him to accuse him of having broken his vow of chastity by having had sexual relationships with her. The Buddha replied, "Sister, only you and I know that you are speaking falsely."

Two versions of what happened next are told in the

commentaries. One version has it that the earth opened and swallowed Chinca into the depths of hell. The other version has it that a heavy block of wood which she had concealed under her robe in order to simulate pregnancy suddenly fell and cut off her toes. In either case, the townspeople knew that Chinca had falsely accused the Buddha, and dismissed her.

Then yet another plot was launched to discredit the Buddha, with dire consequences for the plotters. This time it was a woman named Sundari who was persuaded to claim that she had been spending nights in carnal relationships with the Buddha. After she had made her accusations the plotters killed her and left her body at the monastery, claiming that monks had killed her to protect the Buddha's name. The King dispatched his men to investigate. They found the plotters drinking heavily and arguing among themselves about Sundari's murder. When the plotters were brought before the King they confessed the murder and were duly punished for their crime.

The Buddha, when told about the plot and the false accusations, said, one who lies must accept the consequences of one's *karma*.

And now another serious problem arose, one initiated by a monk of Kosambi named Magandiya who committed a serious violation of the *Patimokkha*, the rules and regulations of the monastic order. All violations of the rules, serious or minor, must be confessed in monastic assembly by the violator, but this monk, believed to have committed the offense, refused to confess it. He was however expelled from the *Sangha*.

The monks then split into two factions, one holding that the monk had done wrong, the other holding that wrongdoing could be expressed only by confession. The arguments became heated, and the Buddha tried to reconcile the two factions by urging patience, union and charity. His words were unheeded, and the Buddha, in great sorrow, withdrew to the forest of Parileyyaka. There he spent a three month period of retreat, "attended by a friendly elephant", until at last the monks came to him, told him they had reconciled, and asked him to pardon them.

The Buddha told the monks that the word *Sangha* meant community, and that it implied living together in a friendly, cordial, compassionate, and understanding manner. He further told them, in explanation of his withdrawal, that a monk who has found "prudent, sober, and wise companions may walk happy; otherwise, rather than be with the unwise, he should walk alone without sin and with few wishes, like the lonely elephant". With these words the Buddha accepted the apologies of the monks, at the same time teaching them a lesson about monastic behavior, and returned to the monastery.

During the following years things went smoothly for the Buddha as he moved from place to place, delivering his discourses, counseling both monks and laypersons, and ever attracting more and more disciples. However, in the fifteenth year of his ministry another unpleasant situation arose for the Buddha, this one created by the Buddha's father-in-law, Suppabuddha, ruler of the Koliya clan.

Suppabuddha, unable to understand or appreciate the motives of a renunciate, had been angered by the Buddha's abandonment of his daughter and grandson, and his anger had grown more and more bitter through the years, climaxing when Yasodhara renounced lay life and became a nun. He now stationed himself in the streets and defied the Buddha, refusing to let him pass, and assailing him with curses. The Buddha turned back but told his attendant

Ananda not to be concerned because within seven days the earth would open and swallow Suppabuddha.

When Suppabuddha was informed of the Buddha's prediction, he secluded himself in his palace. But precisely on the seventh day one of Suppabuddha's horses broke away from the stables and Suppabuddha ran out to stop it. And, as the Buddha had foretold, the earth did open up and Suppabuddha did fall to the lowest depth of hell. The fate of Suppabuddha was not brought about by the Buddha's desire for revenge; the Buddha in his omniscience and clairvoyance had merely foreseen what would inevitably happen to Suppabuddha as a consequence of the bad *karma* brought about by his curses and his defiant behavior.

The most flagrant case of defiance occurred late in the Buddha's life, eight years before his death: the attempt by his cousin Dewadatta[14] to take over his position as leader of the *Sangha*. When the Buddha refused, Dewadatta conspired with Prince Ajatasattu, son of King Bimbisara, the Buddha's protector, to seize control. Ajatasattu was to kill his father and assume the temporal throne, while Dewadatta was to kill the Buddha and assume spiritual authority.

Dewadatta hired a group of sixteen assassins — archers provided by Prince Ajatasattu — to stalk the Buddha as he walked in lonely places. When the would-be assassins,

---

[14] Conflict between Gotama and Dewadatta began many years before when the young cousins were strolling in the woods and Dewadatta shot a swan with his bow and arrow. The future Buddha rushed to extract the arrow and thereby saved the swan's life. Dewadatta then claimed the swan but Gotama refused to give it to him. A wise man who was asked to adjudicate ruled that the swan was the property of the one who had saved its life not the one who had sought to destroy it.

singly or in pairs, successively approached the Buddha, they were overcome with fear, threw down their weapons and confessed their intentions. The Buddha allayed their fears, put them at ease, and converted them.

Dewadatta then climbed to the top of a mountain and released an enormous boulder intended to kill the Buddha as he was walking on a path. The boulder disintegrated before it reached the Buddha but splinters of rock struck him in the foot and drew blood. Knowing that Dewadatta was responsible, the Buddha called out that his cousin had earned great demerit.

Nonetheless, Dewadatta was to try one more time. He let loose a wild elephant on a path where the Buddha was walking, but when the elephant saw the Buddha and sensed his loving-kindness for all sentient beings, he became gentle and subdued, allowing the Buddha to pass unharmed.

Unable to assassinate the Buddha, Dewadatta now came to him and asked that five changes be made in the rules of Sangha, namely that monks must dwell only in the forest, and at the foot of a tree, that they should not accept robes from a layperson and should not accept invitations to be fed at a layperson's house, and that they should be forbidden to eat flesh or fish.

The Buddha said he would not make these rules compulsory, but that they were permissible, with one exception: during the rainy season monks should sleep under a roof. Dewadatta thereupon left the *Sangha* and persuaded five hundred monks to leave with him. The Buddha dispatched Sariputta and Moggallana to prevail on the dissident monks to return, which they succeeded in doing, thus ending Dewadatta's attempt at schism.

Subsequently Prince Ajatasattu became a supporter of the Buddha.

Dewadatta fell ill and after suffering for nine months sent word that he wanted to see the Buddha. His request, according to some commentaries, was refused, but he had himself carried on a litter to the monastery, Jetavana, and when he reached the gate he died and sank to hell. According to other commentaries his request was granted and the Buddha readmitted him to the *Sangha*.

It is a Buddhist belief that many Buddhas preceded Gotama Buddha, that many Buddhas will follow him (and that his immediate successor will be Maitreya). A surprising note to conclude the story of Dewadatta is that the Buddha is reported to have made a prophecy that Dewadatta, "after ten thousand cycles" during which he would have eventually replaced his bad *karma* with good *karma* would be reborn as a Buddha.

CHAPTER SIXTEEN

PARABLES AND INSPIRATION

In addition to the Buddha's teachings as recorded in the *Tripitaka*-preserved discourses, many stories and parables about the Buddha's inspirational wisdom and infinite compassion in his everyday dealings with monks and laypersons have been recorded in the Commentaries, as follows:

ADVICE FOR RAHULA

After Rahula was ordained, the Buddha would preach privately to him. In one of the sessions with his son the Buddha gave him this advice: Practice kindliness, Rahula, so that all enmity will be abandoned. Practice compassion so that all vexation will be abandoned. Practice sympathy so that all aversion will be abandoned. Practice equanimity so that all repulsion will be abandoned. Meditate on the ugly so that lust will be abandoned. And meditate on the impermanent so that pride of self will be abandoned.

PARABLE OF THE MUSTARD SEEDS

When Kisa Gotami's first-born died at an early age, the young mother was so distraught that she went around holding his body in his arms and asking people for medicine to restore him to life. A wise man took pity on Gotami and sent her to see the Buddha.

The Buddha told her that she had done the right thing in coming to him for medicine, and that she should now make the rounds of the entire city and bring back to him grains of mustard seed from a house where no one had ever died. From house to house she went, but she was unable to find one house that death had not visited.

When she returned to the Buddha, he asked if she had come with the mustard seeds. She replied that she had given up looking for them, having learned the lesson the Buddha had taught her: "death is a law common to all mankind". She said that she would arrange for her son's cremation, and that she now desired to learn more about the *Dhamma*. She was thereupon ordained.

THE PARABLE OF THE SOWER

One day when the Buddha was making an alms-round, bowl in hands, he came across a wealthy brahmin landowner who refused to put food in the Buddha's bowl, saying, I plough and sow in order to have food for myself, if you were to do so you would have food to eat.

The Buddha gently replied that he too ploughed and sowed, and having done so he had food to eat.

The brahmin shook his head and asked, where are your bullocks? Where is the seed? Where is the plough?

The Buddha answered, the seed I sow is faith, and good works are as the rain that nourishes it. The plough consists of wisdom and modesty, and my mind is the guiding rein. I lay hold of the handle of the *Dhamma*, I use earnestness as the goad, and my draught ox is diligence. Thus I plough destroying the weeds of delusion. The harvest is *nirvana* by which all sorrow ends.

The brahmin was so impressed that he asked for further instruction, and was accepted as a disciple.

THE HUNGRY MAN

It was the practice of the Buddha when he had been invited to a layperson's house for a pre-noon meal to offer thanks after the meal by delivering a discourse. (Today this custom is yet observed by monks.) One day, at Alavi, a farmer who had intended to pay his respects to the Buddha and attend his after-meal sermon had to go off in search of a wandering ox. It took him all day before he found the animal, and then he hurried to see the Buddha, hoping that he might still be there.

To his surprise, the Buddha was still there, waiting for him. To his further surprise, the Buddha requested that the hungry farmer be fed before delivering his discourse. Some of the monks who accompanied the Buddha wondered why he had done this, and he told them that there is no affliction like hunger, that if the farmer had not been fed he would not have been able to comprehend and benefit from the discourse. (It is said that the omniscient Buddha, who every morning "observed the world", had that morning "observed" that this farmer of Alavi was ready to follow the path.)

The farmer listened attentively to the discourse — on the Four Noble Truths — and decided to become a disciple, to be ordained, and to follow the path.

THE ABUSIVE BRAHMIN

It happened that a brahmin of the Bharadvaja clan one day was behaving angrily and abusively toward the Buddha. Those present were shocked but the Buddha remained calm. He quietly asked the brahmin if he sometimes had guests come to his house. The brahmin brusquely said, yes. The Buddha then asked, "Do you offer your guests hospitality and food?" Again, the brusque answer was, yes. "If your guests do not accept your hospitality and food, what happens to it?" The brahmin answered, "Well, of course, then it remains with me."

"Just so," said the Buddha, "with your anger, your reviling, and your abuse. We do not accept this from you, and so it remains only with you... only with you."

The brahmin was so taken aback that he asked to be forgiven and to be admitted as a monastic disciple. Later he attained enlightenment.

THE DISEASED MONK

One day when the Buddha accompanied by Ananda was visiting a monastery he came across a monk named Tissa lying alone in his room, his skin covered with a loathsome disease, and about him a terrible stench of the diarrhea from which he was also suffering. He lay in pain and misery, solitary and unattended.

The Buddha and Ananda boiled water and bathed the sick monk. They lifted him from his filthy bed and carried him to a clean one. They clothed him in dry garments and when Tissa was feeling refreshed of body and calm of mind, the Buddha preached to him about the "loathsomeness of the body", about its impermanence, and about *nirvana.* Tissa thus attained enlightenment and died an *arahant.*

The Buddha then summoned all the monks of the monastery and preached to them, telling them that in true compassion and loving kindness they must always attend the sick and the suffering.

THE STORY OF ANGULIMALA

"Finger-garland" was what Angulimala was called because he was a villainous murderer who wore around his neck a garland of his victims' fingers. One day when the Buddha was walking on the road, he was warned by the villagers that the infamous murderer was waiting in ambush farther ahead. They urged the Buddha to turn back, but the Buddha "went on in silence".

Angulimala waited until the Buddha passed. Then, holding his sword and shield, he followed the Buddha, intent on taking his life. No matter how fast he walked, nor how fast he ran, Angulimala could not catch up with the Buddha, who was walking at a normal pace.

In frustration Angulimala called out, "Stop, monk! Stop!"

The Buddha answered, "I have stopped. It is you, Angulimala, who have not yet stopped."

Astonished by the answer, and unaware of its implications, the murderer asked, "What is the meaning of what you say?"

The Buddha answered, "Angulimala, I have stopped, stopped forever doing violence to any living being. But you have not yet stopped, you have no restraint."

The murderer stood still in his tracks, looked with awe at the Buddha, and acknowledged the meaning of his words. Together the Buddha and the murderer returned to the monastery, where the murderer requested and was granted ordination as a monk.

Angulimala followed the path and practiced with great diligence, but one morning when he went into the village for alms, he was struck by a clod, a stick, and a potsherd thrown by villagers who recalled his villainous behavior in the past. His bowl was broken, his outer robe was torn, and blood was streaming from his head. In distress he went to the Buddha, who told him not to despair, and said that actually he was quite fortunate to be paying the consequences of his previous bad *karma* in that manner rather than paying for it in hell over many a millenium.

In time the now venerable Angulimala, having been shown the path to enlightenment through the instructions and the loving kindness and compassion of the Buddha, became an *arahant* and attained *nirvana*.

CHAPTER SEVENTEEN

OLD AGE, ILLNESS, AND DEATH

In his eightieth year, in the village of Beluva where he had gone to spend the Rains Retreat, the Buddha was stricken by a serious illness, the nature of which is not known.

Seeing that the Buddha was so ill, Mara, who had not troubled him for many years, came to him and said, it's time now for you to attain final *nirvana*. The Buddha replied that he would not do so until he had "given security to the afflicted", until he saw Buddhism "flourish-ing, held by many, and well proclaimed." Mara said, these things have already come to pass, and the Buddha, having had the satisfaction of hearing Mara testify that he had succeeded in his mission, told the Evil One that he would attain the final *nirvana* in three months' time.

Mara then departed, knowing that evil would persist in the world even though the Buddha had taught the way to purification. Mara knew that some people, perhaps many, would attain enlightenment by following the Buddha's path, whereas others, many more, would not attain enlightenment because they would be addicted and attached to the evils which Mara symbolized.

The moment the Buddha declared that he would pass away in three months' time the earth staggered, great bolts of lightning fell from the sky, mountains toppled, and heavenly drums thundered. Ananda saw this commotion and asked the Buddha what had caused it. The Buddha said that even though he might have chosen to remain alive "for a cycle" he was tired "as an old cart kept together with thongs", that he was worn and ill, and had decided that he would sustain his life for three more months only. He told Ananda that one of the occasions when earthquakes occurred, as this one had, was when a Buddha "shakes off the sum of his life".

The sad news alarmed Ananda and he wept. He asked the Buddha what would happen to the *Sangha* after his death, whom could the disciples turn to for instruction and inspiration? The Buddha answered that the disciples had learned from him everything he was able to teach them and that now they should "dwell as having refuges in themselves and not elsewhere, as having refuges in the Doctrine and not elsewhere."

Ananda then asked what those disciples should do who had become accustomed to pay reverence to the Buddha when the Rain Seasons had ended. The Buddha told him that there were four places to which faithful disciples might go, places that would rouse their devotion: where the Buddha was born, where he attained enlightenment, where he delivered the first discourse on the Turning of the Wheel of the Doctrine, and where he would soon attain complete *nirvana* — Lumbini Grove, Bodhgaya, Benares, and Kusinara, now the four most holy places of Buddhism.

After the Rains Retreat, and despite his serious illness, the Buddha spent his next three months walking slowly and painfully from village to village addressing assemblages of monks and urging them to practice the doctrines he had taught them, "in order that this religion may last long and be perpetuated for the good and happiness of the great multitudes".

When the Buddha arrived at Pava, on what was to be the last day of his life, he stayed in the mango grove of a smith named Cunda, who prepared for him a meal of "hard and soft food" and a serving of *sukaramaddava*. Scholars have been unable to agree on the precise meaning of *sukaramaddava*, some believing that it means soft food of a pig, others that it means soft food given to a pig, mushrooms. Whatever the food may have been, it made the Buddha dreadfully ill, causing him hemorrhages and violent pains.

Through the force of mindfulness and meditation the Buddha was able to control the pains, and he and his faithful attendant Ananda started on their way to Kusinara. On the way the Buddha sat down to rest near a stream, and asked Ananda to bring him water from the stream. Ananda returned empty-handed and told him that the water was not drinkable, that it was muddy and turbid. The Buddha asked Ananda to go back to the stream, and when Ananda did so he found that the water, thanks to the Buddha's wondrous powers, was now clear and pure.

In his compassion, the Buddha, sensing that Cunda might be feeling guilt and remorse, told Ananda to inform Cunda that in a future birth he would receive a great reward. Two gifts, he said, will be blessed above all others: the food given him by Sujata, which revived him so that he could attain Buddahood under the bodhi-tree, and the food given him by Cunda, which brought about his ultimate *Nirvana*.

Proceeding to a grove outside Kusinara, the Buddha lay down for the last time, asking Ananda to arrange a bed with his head to the north. He then arranged himself in "the lion position" on his right side, and seeing that an elder monk was standing in front of him and fanning him, he asked the monk to step aside. He explained that a multitude of gods had assembled to see him and that the elderly monk was obstructing their view.

The Buddha then sent Ananda to the villagers of Kusinara with his compassionate invitation to come see him and be presented to him for the last time. So many came that they could not be presented individually, and Ananda had to ask them to come to the Buddha a family at a time.

His next act of compassion was to assemble the monks and speak to them about the insight and kindness of Ananda. He told Ananda not to weep, reminded Ananda of what he had so often taught him about the impermanence of all things, and assured Ananda: you have always done well, persevere and you too will be freed from the thirst of life, the chain of ignorance.

Later at night a brahmin philosopher named Subhadda came to see the Buddha hoping that he might be able to ask him some questions about the *Dhamma*. Ananda tried to turn him away lest he disturb the Buddha's final moments, but the ever-compassionate Buddha told Ananda to bring Subhadda to him. Talking to him patiently and quietly, the Buddha was able to resolve Subhadda's doubts, after which Subhadda was admitted to the *Sangha* and eventually attained enlightenment.

Then the Buddha asked the five hundred assembled monks if any of them had doubts, misgivings, or questions about any matter of the *Dhamma*. All were silent, and when Ananda expressed his surprise, the Buddha told him that it was not surprising because all the monks present had truly entered the path, had understood his teachings, and were now certainly destined for enlightenment.

With his last breath, the Buddha addressed this final advice to his disciples: "Decay is inherent in all compound things. Work out your salvation with diligence."

Then, as the Buddha entered *parinirvana*, the final *nirvana*, lotus blossoms fell from heaven and covered his body.

PART THREE
THE SANGHA

CHAPTER EIGHTEEN

THE SANGHA, OVERALL

The oldest monastic order in the world came into existence some two thousand five hundred years ago in Northern India when, as we have read, Siddartha Gotama, having attained enlightenment as the Buddha, welcomed a small group of disciples into the *Sangha* and taught them how to follow the path to purification: Enlightenment, and *Nirvana*.

Over the years the *Sangha* grew and thrived, spreading from country to country throughout the East and in recent years into the Western world. One country in which the *Sangha* took early root and grew ever stronger was Siam, the country now known as Thailand, where it is one of the nation's most vital forces. Buddhism is the state religion, the King is its "protector", and the monks of the *Sangha* are its bulwark.

It is impossible to state exactly how many monks there are at any given time, in Thailand or any Buddhist land, because the *Sangha* is ever in flux, with men robing and disrobing. In 1990 in Thailand, however, according to the Department of Religious Affairs there were 187,500 monks and 102,800 novices. During *Pansa*, the rains retreat, the numbers increased to 294,000 monks and 129,600 novices. In other words, 106,500 Thai men were ordained as monks and 26,800 as novices temporarily for the rainy season.

Therava Buddhist monkhood takes many forms. There are short-term monks, long-term dedicated monks, monks who spend much of their time in solitary seclusion, monks who dwell together in large urban monasteries, in small village monasteries, in remote forest monasteries. In any case, for however long they choose to remain in robes, however they choose to practice, and wherever, they have set themselves on the pathway to purification, enlightenment and *nirvana*, some to take only a few steps on the path, others to follow it for a lifetime.

Bhikkhu is the Pali word for monk. It means mendicant. Although the *bhikkhu* has renounced the lay world he is dependent on it and is mendicant in his reliance on laypersons for his sustenance — his food, his robes, his alms-bowl, his necessities. Even his monastery and his lodgings must be built by lay-persons. In turn, the Buddhist lay world is dependent on the *bhikkhu* and the monastic community — for spiritual guidance, for the maintenance and preservation of the Buddhist teachings, for ceremonial rites and rituals, for administering the precepts, and, very importantly, for providing a medium of merit-making.

Merit-making induces good *karma*, which is believed to induce not only a better life in the future but also a propitious form of rebirth. One makes merit in the following ways: generosity (especially toward the *Sangha*), loving-kindness, compassion, moral conduct, meditation, reverence toward and service of parents, teachers, and monks; dedication of one's merit to others, rejoicing in merit made by others; listening to *Dhamma*, reading it, or thinking about it; straightening out one's views through insight-wisdom.

SHORT-TERM MONKS

A Theravada Buddhist monk does not take a lifetime vow; he may disrobe at will. A man may enter and leave monastic life as often as he wishes; however, more often than three times is frowned upon in Thailand. He may wear the robes for as brief a period as a few days, and in some cases, such as at the death of a parent, grandparent or other relative, for even one day. It is usually young male children who wear the robes (of a novice) for one day as a way of making merit for the deceased relative.

Many Thai males elect to be ordained only for the duration of the three-month rainy season (*Vassa*, the rains retreat, also known as the Buddhist Lent) called, in Thai, *Pansa*, after which they will disrobe. This is a way for a male to earn great merit, for himself and for his parents, especially for his mother, as well as an opportunity for him to study the Buddhist teachings, and to meditate. For this temporary service in the monkhood, although it is understood that he will not become a full-time monk, he is nonetheless admired and respected; in fact, a man who has never served as a monk, even if only for the *Pansa* period, is referred to as *dip*, the Thai word for unripe, raw, or immature.

Governmental agencies allow civil servants to take a three-month paid leave of absence while they wear the robes during *Pansa*. Business organizations also allow leaves of absence but where the pressure of work is especially intense, they may be able to release employees for only two or three weeks.

Short-term monks do not permanently renounce lay life, family life, sexual relations, or society. They merely take a leave of absence, knowing that they will resume their normal lives when they disrobe. For these temporary monks the reward is reflected in the respect of their peers and in the conduct of their subsequent lay lives. They are now regarded as *suk*, ripe, mature, finished. They have a better understanding of *Dhamma*, a greater awareness of the desirability of behaving morally. They have an appreciation of the rewards of meditation. They have earned merit. They are better prepared to fill their future role as caring husband, good parent and conscientious citizen.

There are relatively few Thai men who have never been ordained— either out of a sense of social conformity or, more properly, a desire for spiritual training — but these days the ever-increasing, intensely competitive pressures of earning a livelihood or pursuing a business, professional, or academic career make it difficult for some men to renounce the lay world even temporarily.

NOVICES

Novices ordinarily range in age from 8 to 20. They wear the robes of monks but they are not fully ordained. Through their novitiates these young people are assured of shelter, food, and education — an especially strong motivation for the sons of poor, underprivileged families — as well as a profound initiation and indoctrination into the life of the *Sangha* and the Buddhist teachings. Some choose to be ordained as monks and remain in the robes after they have reached maturity, having by then come to appreciate the spiritual life.

A novice is not properly a member of the *Sangha*. He cannot participate in monastic assemblies concerning discipline and administration. He eats apart from the *bhikkhus*, the ordained monks, even if only a small distance apart. He is expected to observe 10 precepts rather than the 227 precepts (more precisely the rules of discipline) of the monk.

The lay Buddhist, as we have seen, undertakes to observe just five precepts: abstention from taking life, from stealing (literally, from taking what is not offered), from improper sexual conduct, from lying (as well as false and harsh speech), and from intoxicants. On special days, holy days known as *Wan Pra* (the day of the full moon and the eighth day thereafter, and the day of the new moon and the eighth day thereafter) some lay Buddhists undertake eight precepts. The third precept — to refrain from improper sexual conduct — becomes more rigid, abstention from all sexual activity. And the additional precepts are: abstention from eating after midday, from witnessing or participating in performances of music, song, or dance, from using garlands, scents or unguents, and from sleeping on a high, wide, soft bed. (Actually nine precepts, but the last two are regarded as one.)

The Buddhist novice permanently undertakes these same precepts, abstaining, like the monk, not just from improper sexual conduct but from all sexual activities (celibacy being a requirement of the monastic life, which calls for renunciation of all attachments). He also, like the monk, undertakes a tenth precept: abstention from receiving gold or silver (money), or items beyond a certain value.

LONG-TERM MONKS

Most monks, the core of the *Sangha*, are long-term renunciates who donned the robes with the intention of remaining in the monkhood for indefinitely long periods, or for the rest of their lives. Many of the long-term monks, among whom are some of the most revered, began their monastic careers as young novices.

Among the renunciate monks are those who live a reclusive, contemplative existence in small and remote forest temples, and those who live a mostly eremetic existence. The eremites have no permanent monastic residence. They are "wandering" monks, treading lonely paths, with a large special kind of umbrella-tent and mosquito netting their only shelter, with the forests and the jungles, and the caves their places of sanctuary.

Most renunciate monks are not reclusive or eremitic; they are cenobitic, residing with fellow monks and participating in ritual, ceremonial, and communal activities. (Monks cannot vote, however, having renounced civic responsibilities.)

WESTERN MONKS

Ordination is open to *farangs*, foreigners, and many foreign monks are to be found in Thailand and other Buddhist countries: American, British, European, Australian, Sri Lankan, Indian, Burmese, and so on. Most Western monks wear the robes only temporarily — from one year to five years, seldom longer. They disrobe having found inner serenity, spiritual purification, Buddhist wisdom — and they return to lay life enriched by the experience. But many Western monks have worn the robes for many years, some intending to wear them for a lifetime, some even having become acting abbots of temples, although not officially appointed by the *Sangha*.

THE EIGHT REQUISITE POSSESSIONS OF A MONK

A monk must possess the eight so-called requisites: his three robes (outer, upper, under), an alms-bowl (large enough to contain about a gallon and a half), needle and thread, a razor, a water strainer, a cloth belt. He is also allowed, in addition, to possess a cloth bag, flint and steel, a mosquito net, a mat, blankets, sandals, an umbrella, towels, dishes, a kettle, a cloth sling for his alms-bowl, and a cloth to sit on when doing his devotions.

In the early days of the *Sangha* monks were not allowed to possess money. These days a monk may need money in order to pay for local or distant travel needs, for books, or for other necessary purchases; knowing this, laypersons will often give money, in envelopes, to monks. Some monks ask a layman to accompany them in order to handle money transactions when they make purchases, but most do so themselves. Those monks who do not wish to possess money deposit it with a lay member of the monastery's congregation to be withdrawn when needed.

While the individual monk may not have possessions other than those mentioned above, the community of monks may. In their desire to earn merit some laypersons give large amounts of money, property, land, houses, vehicles, and other items of considerable value to their favorite temples. (Some Buddhists regard this as unfortunate, improper, and potentially conducive to corruption.)

APPEARANCE OF MONKS

In their renunciation of lay life and its outward manifestations, monks and novices shave their head hair and facial hair (and in Thailand their eyebrows). They shave on the day before the full moon or the new moon (and some shave on both days). They wear orange, saffron, yellow, or brown robes (colors seldom worn in the Buddha's day by laypersons). The various colors of the robes do not signify differences in rank, practice or sect; the color is a matter of personal preference, or has been chosen by the layperson who has donated the robes.

THE MONK AND THE LAITY

Monks conduct worship services for their lay congregations and participate in lay ceremonies outside the temple — merit-making occasions, house blessings, dedications, funerals, cremations. Some monks are heads of orphanages and drug-rehabilitation centers. Some assist, and often supervise, ecological activities, such as tree-planting and other forms of environmental preservation. Some help villagers form farming, marketing, or financial cooperatives, and help them build dams, roads and other facilities.

A Buddhist monk is not a priest. He has no ministry. He does not listen to the confessions of laypersons, does not administer communion, does not baptize, does not christen, does not officiate at weddings. He is not an intercessor between the laity and a God. What's more, a Buddhist monk does not directly proselytize or covertly try to convert members of other religions; he influences only by example and by teachings. (The Buddha, remember, taught that a Buddhist should respect all religions and their practitioners.)

A monk does, however, participate in certain ministerial-like functions. He counsels laypersons on religious and personal matters; if a senior monk he teaches the *Dhamma*, administers the precepts, and, if qualified by the *Sangha's* Council of Elders to do so, he presides over ordinations.

Monks conduct worship services on holidays, on state occasions, on *Wan Pra* days, and on the sacred occasions commemorating significant events in the life of the Buddha. One such is *Makha Bucha*, third month of the full moon cycle, which commemorates the anniversary of the spontaneous gathering of 1,250 *Arahants* before the Buddha, at which time he gave the first recitation of the *Patimokkha*, the rules and regulations of the monastic order. Another is *Visakha Bucha*, sixth lunar month, the anniversary of the birth, the enlightenment, and the death of the Buddha. A third is *Asala Bucha*, eight lunar month, in commemoration of the Buddha's first five disciples (the birth of the *Sangha*) and his first discourse (*sutta*), on the Setting in Motion of the Wheel of *Dhamma*.

On *Makha Bucha*, *Visakha Bucha*, and *Asala Bucha* laypersons gather at their temple to earn merit by offering food in the morning and then to listen to monks in the evening preaching the *Dhamma*, to affirm their devotion to the Triple Gem, to recite the Buddhist precepts, to meditate in silence for several minutes with the monks, and to walk clockwise behind the monks around the *vihara* or the *chedi* three times, holding in tented hands at chest level a lighted candle, three incense sticks, and a floral offering, all of which they then offer to the Buddha images of the temple.

The flowers are symbolic of the beautiful qualities of the Buddha, the candlelight of the *Dhamma* lighting up dark places of the mind and heart, and the incense of the pervasive and influential "fragrance" of the *Sangha*.

MAGIC, ASTROLOGY, FORTUNE-TELLING, AMULETS

The Pali canon prohibits monks from practicing astrology, sorcery, and divination, but in Thailand these prohibitions — which are however not proscribed as offences among the official 227 monastic precepts — are overlooked, especially in the case of astrology. Most Thais, predominantly villagers and farmers, have a tradition of animism, a belief in spirits and the supernatural, and many Thais — including such urban sophisticates as distinguished politicians, statesmen, military leaders and business executives — look to astrological counsel on significant occasions in their lives. Some senior Thai monks, responding to the desires, needs, and traditions of Thai laypersons, practice astrology and give advice based on chart readings. Some monks dispense protective charms and amulets[15] , and exorcise spirits, and monks even participate in certain Brahmanic, non-Buddhist ceremonies such as the Ceremony to Invoke Rain, an important ritual in a land frequently suffering from drought and dependent on rain for abundant crops, especially of its prime source of food, rice.

---

[15] Strict adherents of Buddhism hold that it's all right to wear amulets as long as one regards them reverently as reminders of the Buddha (or of the saintly monks whose images they represent) rather than superstitiously as protective charms or magic charms that will bring the wearer wealth, sex, status, power, and the like.

MONASTIC HIERARCHY

In Thailand the Buddhist ecclesiastical hierarchy is headed by the Supreme Patriarch who is chosen from among the members of the Council of Elders and then appointed by the King. The functions of the ecclesiastical hierarchy parallel those of the state, with senior monks at its summit responsible for overall executive, legislative, and judicial functions, and with ecclesiastical governors in every region, province, and district, who are responsible for those functions which have been delegated to them.

The ecclesiastical hierarchy is autonomous in its conduct of the affairs of the *Sangha*, but is obliged to observe Thailand's laws, and liaisons with the state through the Department of Religious Affairs.

Monasteries rule themselves autonomously, having only one recognized authority, the abbot (who may have one or more assistants, sub-abbots), and who is chosen by the congregation and ratified by ecclesiastical superiors.

TWO MAJOR MONASTIC GROUPS IN THAILAND

The majority of Thai monks are members of the traditional *Mahanikai* order; a minority (maybe 5%) are members of the *Thammayut*, the order founded by King Mongkut (Rama IV) before he was crowned and when he was abbot of Wat Bovornivet Viharn. There is no schism between the two orders, no substantive differences; some members of the younger *Thammayut* order observe, however, a more rigorous discipline, and wear their robes in a special manner.

LAY BEHAVIOR TOWARD MONKS

A monk is greeted by laypersons with the hands held together respectfully in front of the face, an attitude called in Thai a *wai*; a monk does not return the *wai*, as a layperson does when so greeted by another, but may respond with a few words of greeting or with a smile.

A special form of respectful greeting is to prostrate oneself before the monk and touch one's head and hands to the floor three times (as one does before a Buddha image). This special address is sometimes accorded to monastic *achaans* (teachers) by their disciples, and to revered senior monks.

Monks who have worn the robes for ten years, ten consecutive *Vassas*, are known as *Theras*, elders, and have the title "venerable". A monk is referred to as *Pra*, an honorific denoting a higher status, and, depending on his age, is addressed by Thais as *luang phu*,grandfather, *luang pho*, father, or *luang phi*, brother.

A layperson does not shake hands with or embrace a monk; a laywoman maintains a discreet distance from a monk. In gatherings with laypersons a monk is always seated separately in a higher position. When offering food or gifts to a monk a layman places them directly into his hands while a laywoman places them on a piece of cloth in front of his hands.

Even the King of Thailand, Bhumipol Adulyadej, revered and exalted monarch, who is the "protector, defender, and patron of the *Sangha*", and who was himself ordained in 1956 and wore the robes for a fortnight at Wat Bovornivet Viharn, shows his respect for monks by observing the lay protocols of behavior toward them, including greeting them with a *wai* and assuming a physically inferior position in their presence.

Despite these proprieties of behavior the layperson need not feel intimidated in the presence of a monk, as some Westerners do. One can and should feel perfectly at ease and need only be respectful by observing the proprieties. Westerners should realize, as all Buddhists do, that a monk is a man of compassion, good will, loving-kindness, sympathy, and understanding. He does not intimidate. He welcomes conversation with laypersons.

CHAPTER NINETEEN

TEMPLE-MONASTERIES

Among a Buddhist land's greatest glories are its temple-monasteries, distinctive and splendid in their architecture and art, meaningful in the spiritual and ritual lives of all lay Buddhists, hallowed sanctuaries where resident monks and nuns follow the path.

Most visitors to Thailand are familiar with certain magnificent *wats* in Bangkok, most notably the Temple of the Emerald Buddha[16] in the Royal Palace compound *(Wat Pra Kaew)*, the Temple of the Reclining Buddha *(Wat Po)*, the Marble Temple *(Wat Benchamabopit)*, the Temple of the Dawn *(Wat Arun)*. The splendor of such temples is manifest in their elegant multi-tiered roofs, in their dazzling ornamentation, their gilded stupas, their striking statuaries, their artistic murals, their marvelous Buddha images.

Throughout Thailand there are similarly resplendent temples, those in the cities outside Bangkok perhaps not so ornate as the most famous Bangkok temples, but places of

---

[16] *Wat Pra Kaew*, the most revered of all Thai temples and housing Thailand's most venerated Buddha image, the Emerald Buddha, is not a residence of monks, although on religious holidays worship services are conducted there.

splendor and beauty, and those in the villages — even the poorest villages — as beautiful and ornamental as the villagers' limited means can afford. Many centuries-old temples are notable for their very simplicity, with wooden structures of immense charm, and with their interiors containing extraordinary murals, precious antiques, and sacred artifacts.

On a ride through the Thai countryside the visitor suddenly notices a *wat*[17] high atop a jutting hillside, like a crown on the peak's crest, or one far off the road nestled in a forest or adjacent to a rice field. The adventurous visitor can find *wats* on small remote islands and even in deep jungles.

There are 29,015 temples[18] in Thailand: city, village, and forest temples, and some one hundred "royal" temples which were built or supported by Thailand's monarchs. Temples may differ in architecture, design, ornamentation, and size, but they have certain characteristics in common, in that they contain within their boundaries five basic structures:

1) A *sala*, an open-sided assembly hall used in the villages not only for worship services on those holy days when many people are in attendance, but also as a sort of social and civic center, a school for the lay children, as a polling-place on election days, and even as a place where

---

[17-18] The Thai word *wat* is usually translated for purposes of simplicity as **temple** whereas actually a *wat* is a **compound** consisting not only of temples, but also of other structures, including *salas*, stupas, monastic dwellings, etc., as described on this and the following page. I use the words *wat*, temple, monastery, and temple-monastery interchangeably to indicate such a compound.

travellers can stay overnight sleeping on the floor.

2) A *vihara*, a temple used when laypersons join the monks for religious services and where monks assemble morning and evening for their own communal devotions. Within this temple are an altar on which stand revered Buddha images, mural paintings, and, often, painted or ornamented ceilings.

3) An *uposatha* (in Thai, *bot*), the most sacrosanct building in the *wat*, a temple used primarily by the monks for such *Sangha* ceremonies as ordinations (when laypersons may be present), and confessional recitations (when laypersons cannot be present). The *uposatha* is erected on consecrated ground marked by what are called *sima* stones which are placed beneath the surface of the ground at four cardinal points and four intermediate points of the compass, with other stones placed on the surface to mark the sites. A ninth *sima* is buried in consecrated soil under the floor of the *uposatha*.

(In some villages where the laypersons do not have the funds to erect individual structures, one building serves as *vihara* and *uposatha*, and even in some instances as sala also.)

4) A stupa, *chedi* in Thai, a bell-shaped tower. Some (the most sacred) contain near the base actual relics of the Buddha, while others contain relics of the Buddha's disciples or ashes of royal personages, or even religious documents. All stupas are sacred and revered symbolic representations of the Buddha.

5) Lodging for the monks. In some temples the monks are lodged in a single dormitory-like structure, in others they occupy individual quarters, called *kutis* in Thai. All the lodgings are sparsely furnished, and measure about 8' by 12'.

Large *wats* may contain several additional structures: multiple *chedis*, burial stupas, a building which houses the symbolic "footprint" of the Buddha, a repository for the many volumes of the *Tripitaka* (the Buddhist canon), a gallery or a museum, a school, a crematorium. Some may also have accommodations, far removed from those of the monks, for female renunciates called *Mae Chiis*. Although referred to as "nuns", they are not nuns in the Western, religious sense. They are women who have chosen to follow the path to enlightenment reclusively (without having been fully ordained, since only men may be ordained in Theravada Buddhism); they shave their heads, wear white robes, and, in a partial ordainment undertake to observe eight (or sometimes ten) precepts. Usually, these are women whose children are grown, who are widowed, or who no longer feel family or social obligations.

Some *wats* allow vendors to set up stalls within the compound for the sale of food, refreshments, and souvenirs — *Wat Mahathat* in Bangkok, for example, has so many vendors on its grounds that it resembles a marketplace — although usually vendors locate themselves outside the compound, near the entrance.

Some *wats* also have accommodations for laypersons who wish to learn how to meditate, to study *Dhamma*, and to approximate the experience of monastic life. *A Brief Guide to Buddhist Meditation Centres in Thailand*, published by the National Identity Board, 1988, lists and describes the best-known twenty of them. This is a useful guide which lists meditation-centres in Bangkok and Central Thailand, in the North, Northeast, and South — by name, location, name of teacher, size, description, accommodation, facilities, food, language, daily routine, teaching method, and meditation system. These centres range from the above- mentioned

Wat Mahathat in Bangkok, one of Thailand's largest monasteries (300-400 monks), to *Wat Pang Bua* on Samui Island, one of Thailand's smallest (two monks).

When visiting a temple-monastery one should dress properly, should not wear shorts, and, in the case of women, should not wear immodest dresses or blouses. One should remove one's shoes and doff any head-covering when entering any building which contains a Buddha image — a *vihara,* a *bot,* a *sala* — and when entering a monk's residence. (In some monasteries, as in those of northern Thailand, women are not allowed to enter sacred buildings, and such buildings are clearly identified by signs in both Thai and English.)

One may take photographs in a monastery (except where signs, in English, prohibit doing so) and may photograph monks. As a matter of courtesy one should ask a monk for permission, which is usually granted.

One should not act boisterously or talk raucously lest one disturb the serenity of monks who are meditating or studying. And one should not remove **anything** from a temple, not even a flower or a leaf, and most certainly not any religious artifacts that are often left unattended. Many temples have souvenir counters where visitors may purchase miniature replicas of the Buddha images within, or Buddha amulets, or amulets reproducing the likeness of the abbot, and other items.

Despite these caveats, a temple-monastery is not an austere, forbidding place, just as its resident monks are not. It is a place where one can relax, contemplate, and enjoy the beauty of the temples, the *chedis,* the grounds. Visiting a temple-monastery is a joyous experience for a Buddhist, just as it should be for a non-Buddhist Westerner.

Indeed, whether Buddhist or not, Westerner visitors to

a temple who wish to do so — and many do, although it is not mandatory — may demonstrate their respect for the Triple Gem of Buddhism by offering at the base of the altar a lighted candle, three incense sticks and flowers, which are usually available at a cost of just a few bahts (twenty cents). Sometimes a packet of gold leaf is included, the leaf to be applied to a Buddha image.

Entrance to most temples is free; a few, very few, charge a modest admission fee. However, a Western visitor may wish to make a contribution to the maintenance of facilities or the construction of facilities and other amenities for its resident monks. Contribution boxes are provided for this purpose, silent reminders that the monastery and its monks are totally dependent on the beneficence of the layperson.

****

The Buddha described a "favorable" monastery as having five characteristics: 1) not too far from, not too near a lay community and with a path for going and coming; 2) little frequented by day, with little sound, and few voices by night; 3) little contact with mosquitoes, flies, wind, burning sun, and creeping things; 4) where robes, alms, food, lodging and medicine are easily obtainable; 5) where elder monks reside who are learned, versed in the Scriptures, observers of the *Dhamma* (Buddhist teachings), observers of the *Vinaya* (the monastic disciplines), and capable of explaining and teaching.

A "favorable" monastery with these characteristics may have been easier for a monk to find in remote northern India in the Buddha's time than in contemporary Thailand. Today the best-known monasteries are "frequented by day" with tourists and with lay Buddhists; the activities of festive temple fairs sometimes run well into the late hours of the night; insects abound in virtually all Thai monasteries, and a "burning sun" is hard to avoid in Thailand's tropical climate. Nonetheless, the monk trains himself to be immune to distractions and noises, and indifferent to insects and the "burning sun".

For the Buddhist monk his monastery — be it in the heart of busy, bustling Bangkok, or in a remote village or island, or in the depth of the forest — is, as the Buddha said, a "lonely place wherein he of peaceful heart sees *Dhamma* rightly and knows a joy not of men", a place where he can follow the pathway to purity, the pathway to enlightenment and *nirvana*.

CHAPTER TWENTY

ORDINATION

"This is the time for honesty. The questions you will now be asked, in the presence of our *Sangha*, should be answered truthfully, without embarrassment, without shame:

"Do you have leprosy?

"Do you have boils?

"Do you have ring worm?

"Do you have tuberculosis?

"Do you have epilepsy?

"Are you a human being?

"Are you a male?

"Are you free of indebtedness?

"Are you released from governmental, military, or royal service?

"Do you have the permission of your parents?

"Are you twenty years of age?

"Have you your bowl and your robes?

"What is your name?

"What is the name of your preceptor *(Upajjhaya)*?"

This interrogation, conducted in Pali, is one of the basic steps in the process of ordination. The questions derive from the time of the Buddha, as may be inferred from those regarding diseases and illnesses which were prevalent then but less so now.

The question, "Are you a human being?" also derives from the time of the Buddha, for legend has it that a *naga*, the mythical water serpent, out of adoration and respect for the Buddha, appeared for ordination in the form of a human being and was expelled only after the truth was discovered. On his expulsion he asked if he might be allowed to make his name a respectful offering to the Buddha. His request was granted, and candidates for ordination are now called *naga*.

The question, "Are you a man?" carries an implication beyond that of mere differentiation of male and female sex. Its intention also is: are you a whole man, in other words, not a eunuch? Buddhist monks should be whole, virile males whose vow of celibacy is thus all the more meaningful.

Before the candidate is interrogated he will have gone to the abbot of the temple, or to an elder monk who has been qualified by the Council of Elders to ordain, and he will have expressed his desire to become a monk. He will have been taught by a monk known as an *achaan* (Thai:teacher) enough Pali to be able to follow the ordination ritual. His hair and eyebrows will have been shaved. He will have acquired monastic robes and an alms-bowl, which are usually provided as an act of merit-making by his relatives or friends.

The occasion of ordination is a profoundly significant one in Buddhist society, not only for the candidate but also for his parents and relatives, to whom, as well as to himself, his ordination brings great merit. The lay ceremonies attending his ordination are frequently, though not necessarily, elaborate: For days prior to his ordination his parents may have sponsored festivities and banquets. In the villages of Thailand neighbors may have accompanied the *naga* to the temple in a triumphant procession on the day of his leaving the secular world, the *naga* riding a horse or an elephant or borne on the shoulders of friends, with a ceremonial umbrella held over his head. Those who participate in the procession will have carried gifts for him and for the monks who conduct the ordination ceremony: robes, flowers, candles, incense, food, and other articles which are useful to the monks.

The candidate for ordination tells the senior monks who have gathered for the occasion in the *bot* that he desires to be admitted to the *Sangha*. In the two-step ceremony that follows he is first accepted as a novice and then, having been told by his *achaan* the rules of the *Sangha*, and the rewards of the monastic life, and having been given instruction concerning the life of a monk, the applicant is given full ordination *(Upasampada)*.

Concluding the ceremony the now-ordained monk presents gifts to his preceptor and his *achaan* and the other senior monks who have officiated, while they chant a blessing. During his ordination he has been given a Pali name, and identification papers afterwards.

Although the lay ceremonies may be elaborate and the monastic ordination ceremonies lengthy and complex (I have given only a brief, simplified description of them), it is relatively easy for a Buddhist man to become a monk. Since Thai Buddhist men, are *expected* to wear the robes,and most do, at some time during their lives, ordination is made readily accessible for them. A candidate for ordination need not undergo extensive training or schooling, he need not have studied at a seminary or spent a length period as a monastic novice, and, as previously mentioned, he need not take irrevocable vows to renounce lay life for the rest of his days.

Unfortunately, with admission for ordination so permissive, the monkhood sometimes attracts idle, lazy, neurotic, or maladjusted individuals; fortunately, since such individuals are unable to live up to the standards of the monastic life — especially the rigid rules and disciplines — their tenure as monks is usually short-lived.

However easy it may be to become a monk, that is to be ordained, it is not easy to be a monk. For once a man dons the robes he commits himself to a life of austerity, of poverty, of chastity, of renunciation of worldy pleasures.

He commits himself to a rigid set of monastic disciplines, the 227 rules of the *Patimokkha*, rules which he **must** follow, and to a rigid code of behavior which he **should** follow, the *Abhisamacara*, training in proper conduct (which will be explained in the next chapter.)

He commits himself to long hours of meditation, to learning several chants and to studying *Dhamma*. He may go on to the difficult study of Pali and of the extensive texts of the *Tripitaka* (the three large volumes containing the Buddhist canon), and he may take the examinations which lead to higher rank in the *Sangha*, as well as to high office in the ecclesiastical hierarchy.

Above all, the man who receives ordination as a monk commits himself to following the pathway to *enlightenment* and *nirvana*.

CHAPTER TWENTY-ONE

RULES AND REGULATIONS

In donning the robes the monk has declared his intentions to renounce lay life, to abandon possessions, to reject all sexual activities and sensual desires, to struggle against ego-enhancement, to resist delusions about self. In order to accomplish these goals he has agreed to enter a unique community in which he not only will practice all aspects of self-improvement but also will live in harmonious, peaceful, considerate and compassionate interrelationship with his fellow monks.

He must learn a new way of life, a new mode of behavior, a new set of rules and regulations quite unlike those of his previous lay life. He must, in order to comport himself properly in this new way of life, learn and abide by the *Vinaya*, which consists of the *Patimokkha* (the 227 precepts — rules of discipline — of monastic life) and of the *Abhisamacara* (training in appropriate conduct).

If a Buddhist layperson fails to observe any of the precepts (only five) there is no imposition of punishment or penance, nor is there absolution through confession. The consequence to a lay Buddhist of not observing the precepts is the accumulation of bad *karma*: good actions have good consequences, bad actions have bad consequences, in this or in subsequent lives. Observance of the precepts is voluntary, not mandatory; violation of the precepts is strictly a personal matter.

Not so with the Buddhist monk: observance of the precepts is mandatory. If he fails to observe his rules of discipline — all 227 — he is subject to expulsion from the *Sangha*, or to disciplinary action, or to suspension or probation, to forfeiture or expiation. Violations of the precepts are called offences *(apatti)*, some of which are regarded as incurable, others curable, but all subject to disciplinary action depending on the gravity of the offence.

The most grave offences are those whose commission results in expulsion. The monk who commits them is regarded as "defeated"; in other words he is no longer a monk and can never be ordained again. There are four such offences: 1) indulging in sexual intercourse, with a female, a male, a hermaphrodite, "even with a female animal"; 2) stealing a thing of such value "that kings would have the robber arrested and either executed, imprisoned or banished"; 3) depriving a human being of life; 4) falsely claiming the attainment of superhuman states like those attained by an *Arahant*, one who is enlightened.

There are thirteen offences which are considered grave enough to require the *Sangha* (which may be a chapter of as few as four monks, no fewer) to order the offender to observe penance and probation: five concern sexual offences short of intercourse — intentional emission of semen, lustfully touching a woman, lustfully addressing a woman, inviting a woman to indulge in sex, and acting as an intermediary between man and woman concerning marriage or living together. Eight concern offences that are detrimental to monastic community life: having *kutis* built of improper dimensions or having them built without permission, falsely accusing a fellow monk of having committed one of the major offences, attempting to cause schism or quarrels, resisting admonishment; flattering or fawning on laypersons, giving them gifts, or living on intimate terms with them so as to cause in them a decline of faith or a loss of respect for the monk himself.

Thirty rules concern the accumulation, possession and use of cloth, robes, sitting rugs, handling of money. Violation of any of these precepts calls for forfeiture and expiation.

Ninety-two offences call for expiation only. Offences regarded as "evil conduct" are lying, slandering, drinking intoxicants. Offences regarded as "cruel conduct" are killing an animal, being abusive, striking a blow, threatening another; offences that cause a "bad reputation" are sitting in a screened place with a woman, lying down in the same place as a woman, travelling with a woman, eavesdropping. Additional offences concern mischievous behavior — tickling, teasing, swimming for pleasure — the improper consumption of foods, as well as bad manners and carelessness.

There are seventy-four additional rules concerning proper conduct. They deal with wearing the robes properly, with behaving properly in inhabited areas, towns and villages, with accepting alms and eating meals, with teaching *Dhamma* to disrespectful laypersons, and even with the manner of urinating and defecating. Violations should be confessed to a fellow (senior) monk, but do not involve monastic discipline.

Finally there are rules governing judicial investigations concerning the conduct of monks.

The above constitute, in brief, the *Patimokkha*, the 227 so-called precepts which a monk *must* observe lest he be faced with expulsion, suspension, expiation, or forfeiture. In addition there are a great many training rules, the *Abhisamacara*, which a monk *should* observe: rules about shaving the hair, rules proscribing the growth of a mustache or beard or letting the nails or nasal hairs grow long, proscribing the wearing of ornaments, proscribing attendance at performances of dancing, singing or music, proscribing gambling, proscribing the making of floral garlands, and so on.

Failure to observe the rules of the *Abhisamacara* carry no punishments. A monk strives to observe them, in addition to those of the *Patimokkha*, in order to improve himself, to be better able to follow the pathway to purity.

Twice a month, on the *Wan Pra (Uposatha)* days of the full moon and the half-moon, monks hold special ceremonies in their *bot*, with no laypersons present, at which the entire *Patimokkha* is recited, and the monks confess any transgressions. Furthermore, it is customary for a junior monk to confess daily (even two or three times daily) to a senior any offences he may have committed in the previous hours. In turn the senior monk then confesses to the junior, and both vow to observe the rules and regulations more rigorously.

It must be acknowledged that some monks violate the rules and regulations and do not confess their transgressions either in assembly or in private. Just as there are those who behave well and those who behave badly in lay life, so it is in monastic life where, as has been noted, it is relatively easy for a man even of loose morality to be ordained. However, men who are not inclined to observe the high moral standards of monkhood do not usually choose to remain long in the *Sangha*, and those few who do misbehave generally face being tried by ecclesiastical courts and ordered to disrobe.

In the main, as expressed in the *Visuddhi Magga* ,"The Path of Purification"[19] : "A monk is respectful, deferential, possessed of conscience and shame, wears his inner robes properly, wears his upper robe properly; his manner inspires confidence, he has deportment, he guards the doors of his sense faculties, knows the right measure in eating, is devoted to wakefulness, possesses mindfulness and full awareness, wants little, is contented, is strenuous, is a careful observer of good behavior, and treats his teachers with great respect." In short, he observes the *Patimokkha* and the *Abhisamacara*.

---

[19] A classic manual of Buddhist doctrine and meditation written in the 5th century by the scholar Buddhaghosa.

CHAPTER TWENTY-TWO

DAILY ROUTINE AND SPECIAL ACTIVITIES

Two hours before the sun appears on the eastern horizon the pealing of the temple bell signals the time, 4 A.M.

The resident monks, having spent the night on a thin mattress under a plain cotton blanket, open their eyes and rise from sleep to start the day. The Buddha said that four hours' sleep should be enough for a monk, but nowadays monks generally sleep at least six hours, and when the bell wakes them, there is no hesitation about rising, no soporific lingering.

The bell also awakens the dogs and cats that have been taken to the monastery by people who no longer want or can afford to keep them as pets, and who know that the monks will feed them and take care of them. (There is hardly a monastery in Thailand that does not have its resident "temple" dogs and cats.)

The temple dogs, awakened by the bell, begin their matutinal howling and maintain it until the pealing fades into silence. Perhaps the dogs resent being awakened that early, or perhaps their howling is an eager response to what they know will soon be the dawn, and that dawn means imminent breakfast. They begin to gather around the monks' residences and the *sala* where the monks will assemble after having made their rounds *(pindapata)* for their early-morning meal.

The temple cats stir, stretch, and go back to sleep; they have more patience than the dogs, or perhaps they're simply wiser, knowing that breakfast awaits the sun's rising over the horizon and is yet two or three hours away.

The monks now perform their morning ablutions and don their outer robes. They kneel before the Buddha images in their lodgings and pay homage to the Buddha. Then, after whatever housekeeping may be required, the monks do their morning meditations, some sitting in their lodgings or just in front of them, in the half-lotus position, others practicing the walking forms of meditation.

When the pre-dawn darkness is dispelled by morning light strong enough so that "one can see the lines in one's palm", 6 A.M. or a little thereafter, the monks leave the monastery grounds to begin their food-gathering rounds.

Although a monk is a mendicant — the word *bhikkhu* actually means beggar — he does not walk the streets with outstretched hands or sit on the pavements; he does not ask for contributions of food, does not overtly beg. On his morning rounds he walks silently, eyes downcast, barefoot, along the lanes and streets of the adjacent neighborhood. He carries his alms bowl, often suspended by a sling across one shoulder.

While on his rounds he thinks about the four sole essentials of monastic life — his robes, his shelter, his medicines, his alms food-bowl — contemplating that his simple robes are merely protection from the elements and from insects, as well as covering for his private parts, that his austere dwelling place is mere protection from the elements, his medicines mere necessities in case of illness, and his bowl a means for obtaining food which is merely for life sustenance, not for pleasurable consumption.

He stops only when he is respectfully and quietly addressed by a layperson waiting at the side of the road to place food offerings in his bowl.

Since it is an important part of Buddhists' belief that they earn merit by their generosity to monks, they place in the monks' alms-bowls ready-to-eat food of the best quality, such as: fragrant rice or sticky rice, barbecued chicken, pork, fish, tasty curries, soups — in plastic bags — cartons of milk, fruit juices, hard-boiled eggs, cakes, cookies, fruits, candies.

(Some monks are vegetarians, although they are not required to be. If meat comes from animals that have not been expressly slaughtered to provide food for them, monks are permitted to eat it.)

When the monks and novices emerge from their monastery around 6 A.M. and walk along the lanes of the adjacent neighborhood they find laypersons, mostly women, waiting with food in front of their houses. (Women cannot earn merit as men can by becoming monks, but they can earn merit in other ways, the most notable of which are having a son ordained and by providing food and other gifts for the monks.)

Some laypersons offer food, sometimes along with flowers, every morning. Some do so only on special occasions, such as birthdays or anniversaries of the deaths of close relatives, loved ones, and even of pets. (Yes, even pets, like all sentient beings, will, Buddhists believe, be reborn; earning merit for them in this way may help bring them a better rebirth.)

By 7:30 the monks have usually completed their rounds. They return to the monastery with (usually) full bowls, sometimes so full that they will have more than enough food for breakfast, with enough left over for an ample second meal. Always food is shared with the *dek wats* (Thai: temple boys), young lay boys who live at the monastery, or stay there during the day, and assist the monks in their housekeeping, in care of the grounds, and in running errands, for which the monks reciprocate by feeding them and by teaching them *Dhamma*. And — food is shared with the temple dogs and the temple cats, as well as with anybody else who happens to be around at meal-time.

After breakfast the monks resume their meditations, or do their morning chanting, or, in the case of the younger monks, attend classes in Buddhist instruction, or spend their time reading, or even take a short nap. (Some monks may nap in the afternoon but excessive napping during the day, a form of slothfulness, is prohibited.)

At approximately 11 A.M. the monks partake of their second meal, finishing it, as prescribed in the Theravada canon, before noon. This will be their last meal of the day, but they are allowed to have liquid refreshments, important to their well-being in a hot climate. Some monks only take one meal a day.

One reason why a monk must not eat after mid-day is that he thus keeps his body "light and comfortable in the afternoon, evening, and night in order to meditate without drowsiness".

Another is that this limitation on eating reduces his craving for food, which, like all cravings, sensual desires and attachments, a monk strives to eliminate. (Smoking, a modern habit, is not prohibited by any of the centuries-old monastic rules and regulations. It is however recognized as an attachment and is discouraged. Some abbots do prohibit smoking.)

In the afternoon friends and relatives may come to visit, but they do not excessively prolong their visits lest they intrude on the monk's time of solitary meditation, or on his attendance at classes, which are conducted by elder monks for the benefit of "new" monks, less than one year in robes, and "middle" monks, fewer than five years. If not attending classes the "new" and "middle" monks may read *Dhamma* on their own or memorize and practice the many chants which are so important to monastic life.

At classes, which may be at their resident temple or elsewhere at monastery schools, monks study the life of the Buddha (real and legendary lives), the Buddha's teachings *(Dhamma)*, and the Rules of Conduct (the *Patimokkha*). Examinations are given in Three Grades, Third through First, and monks who pass their examinations are awarded certificates for each grade in which they have become proficient. Additionally, monks may attend special schools to study Pali, achieving the highest Grade, Nine, or may go to advanced study at a monastic university.

At 5 P.M. the temple bell peals again, this time to summon the monks to evening devotions at the *vihara,* after which "new" and "middle" monks often again attend formal or informal instructional classes. Then all monks retire for further meditation before going to sleep.

As has been previously mentioned, each temple is governed autonomously by its abbot. Some abbots allow their monks to watch TV or listen to music on their radios and cassette players. Others strictly forbid such activities. Some insist on regular hours of meditation. Some insist on attendance at classes and at twice-daily worship services.

The monk's normal routine differs on days when he is engaged in special activities: temple-centered ceremonies, state ceremonies and holidays, home-centered ceremonies, and monastic ritual ceremonies.

An example of temple-centered ceremony is that which takes place during *Songkran*, the traditional Thai New Year, a time of water festivals. A Westerner visiting Thailand during *Songkran*, April 13-14-15, might perceive it merely as an occasion for what the Thais call *sanuk* (having a good time), as evidenced by young Thai men and women gleefully splashing water on passersby. But *Songkran* has a religious significance as evidenced in the ceremonies and rites that take place in the temples.

Laypersons make merit on *Songkran* by bringing food for the temple monks, by sprinkling or bathing the temple's Buddha images, thereby purifying and rejuvenating them for the year ahead, and by bringing sand for the temple grounds to replace sand that may have been unwittingly removed during the previous year on the shoes of visitors. (Nothing should be wittingly removed from a temple.) Thus, *Songkran*, the water festival, is in its religious sense a time of cleansing, a time for a new start made meaningful by the interaction between laypersons and monks, and commemorated by the evening chanting of blessings by the temple monks.

Celebrations of holidays such as the Thai New Year, the King's Birthday, the Queen's Birthday, Coronation Day, Constitution Day, Chulalongkorn Day, and others, include presentation of food to monks, worship services, and chanting by monks.

For home-centered ceremonies monks leave their temples at the invitation of laypersons to be the honored guests and conductors of rituals marking house-warmings, childbirths, birthdays, anniversaries, weddings (but only some time prior to or after the actual wedding ceremonies, which monks are not permitted to attend), and funerals. On these occasions the monks — invited in odd numbers for festive occasions, in even numbers for sad ones (funerals, cremations, memorial services) — chant appropriate blessings or *suttas*, spray lustral water, are fed, and are given various gifts (necessities such as soap, toothpaste, tissue paper, and even money in envelopes).

A precise procedure is followed on these occasions. The monks sit cross-legged on a raised platform, if one is available, or on pillows and mats placed against a wall. One of the household's revered Buddha images has been placed on an altar-stand to the right of the monks, who sit in order of monastic seniority, with the most senior closest to the Buddha image.

A length of unspun cotton yarn — a sacred cord called *sai sin* — has been wound three times around the base of the Buddha image and, on merit-making occasions such as house-blessings, has been passed out of the house, pulled fully around the house, and brought back in to be rolled into a ball and placed on the altar.

As is the case with all Buddhist ceremonies, the ritual begins with a request to the officiating monk by the host, or an honored guest, that he lead the assembled guests in reciting, in Pali chanting, the *Namo*, the Three Refuges, and the Five Precepts.

Next the host will request that the monks intone a sacred chant for the welfare of the assemblage. At a certain point in the ceremony the head monk will unwind the roll of sacred thread and pass it along from monk to monk so that each can hold it in his hand while chanting. This ritual of the *sai sin* connects the monks to the Buddha image, to one another, and to the strand that surrounds the house, thereby blessing everything and everybody within its periphery.

Westerners who have the privilege of attending a household merit-making ceremony and of observing the ceremonies find the occasion inspiring and memorable. (I've explained some of the ceremonial activities so that Westerners who may have occasion to witness them in the future will better understand their significance.)

During the course of the year there are several monastic ritual ceremonies of special significance. Perhaps the most important is the ritual of *Khao Pansa*, entering the three-month retreat during the rainy season beginning in mid-July and ending in mid-October, (*Vassa* in Pali), and referred to by some as the Buddhist Lent although it bears no similarity to the Christian Lent.

During *Pansa* the normal resident population of every temple-monastery is greatly increased by the presence of new monks who come to wear the robes and live the monastic life only temporarily. (At some temples the monk population is virtually doubled during *Pansa*.) A special ceremony is held generally during the afternoon on the first day of *Pansa*, the day of "taking up residence" for the rains retreat, at which all the monks chant vows to live in harmony with one another, to share what they have with one another, not to let quarrels arise and not to annoy others by behaving improperly or by expressing wrong opinions.

Although the ceremony is intended primarily as a kind of introduction for the new monks it also serves to remind the long- term monks that living together as a community — *Sangha* in Pali literally means community — under abnormally crowded conditions for three months requires good will, patience, good behavior, mutual consideration, mutual affection, mutual respect and mutual helpfulness.

Concluding this ceremony is another called *Pavarana*,

when the young monks ask their elders to forgive them if they have misbehaved toward them in any way, and the elder monks then similarly beg the forgiveness of their juniors. No grudges are to be carried into the future so that all the monks can take up residence in a spirit of complete harmony during the *Pansa* period or later when going on to other pursuits.

Aside from its exclusively monastic aspects, *Pansa* is also a time of lay involvement. On the first day of *Pansa* laypersons present food, flowers, incense and candles to the monks, and during the following three-month period they are especially generous in their donations of food and other benefactions. It is also a time when laypersons will make frequent visits to their sons, grandsons, or other relatives who are wearing the robes.

At the end of *Pansa* all the monks again hold a ceremony of *Pavarana* on the day called *Ok Pansa*, the day of leaving the rain retreat. The short-term monks prepare to disrobe and leave the monasteries, some remaining there until they can participate in the *Tot Kathin* ceremony or take the ecclesiastical examination for the first certificate of Buddhist studies.

Tot Kathin, which follows *Ok Pansa*, is a month-long period of special merit-making for laypersons during which they demonstrate their great esteem for the long-term monks by presenting them with robes and other gifts. It is a time when groups of Buddhists — social groups, employees of a company, or entire village communities — select a particular temple for their benefactions, sometimes travelling long distances, as, for example, from Bangkok to Chiang Mai. For such groups, whether travelling together by bus, train, or boat, the pilgrimage is one of *sanuk*, having a good time, as well as for merit-making.

The abbot of the selected temple, having been previously notified, assembles his monks for this festive and joyous occasion, and selects a monk who has behaved well in practice and discipline to accept the *Kathin* robes for subsequent distribution. The monks chant blessings for the donors.

During the *Tot Kathin* period, as well as on other auspicious occasions, the King and Queen and members of the royal family visit what have been designated as royal temples where they too present *Kathin* robes and other gifts.

Thus, on these occasions and others, participation in monastic ceremonies by the laity (including royalty) and participation in lay ceremonies by the monks constitute what may be called the "warp and woof" of a Buddhist nation — indivisible strands in a texture of ritual and spiritual communion. Indeed, the word *Sangha* is used to describe not only the monastic order itself but also the communal "togetherness" of Buddhist monks and Buddhist laypersons.

CHAPTER TWENTY-THREE

CHANTING

A monk chants when engaged in his private devotions and meditations. He chants during worship services, during state and holiday ceremonies, during house ceremonies. He chants at ordination ceremonies, and he chants on many other occasions: after receiving alms, while dedicating temple buildings and Buddha images, offering blessings to laypersons, praying for the deceased at funeral services and at cremations, at merit-making festivals, at rain-invocation ceremonies, and so on and so on.

In short, chanting is an ancient, basic and indispensable part of the monastic life, a communicative and aesthetic form of monastic language.

The Buddhist monastic university Mahamakut Rajavidyalaya — one of the two monastic universities in Bangkok, the other being Mahachulalongkorn Raja-vidyalaya — has published a book entitled *Pali Chanting with Translations* which contains the chants a monk or novice "will need to know for use in the *wat* and in invitations to the houses of lay people". About 55 different chants are included —for the precepts, for the refuges, for protective blessings, for dedications, for making merit for the dead, for chanting after eating, and for use on other occasions. And these are only a small portion of the chanted discourses and verses and *Suttas* (various forms of *Dhamma* teachings) and stories about the Buddha's previous lives that constitute the entire body of Buddhist Pali chants. *The Royal Book of Chants*, 403 pages, contains more than 200 chants!

The most frequently memorized and recited chants are those which are chanted at morning and evening services, those recited during merit-making rites at the temple in which laypersons participate, those recited after having been given food or other gifts by laypersons, those recited at the houses of laypersons on auspicious occasions such as house-blessings, and inauspicious occasions such as immediately after a person dies.

Clearly, only the long-term monk can be expected to be proficient in having memorized and in reciting the many chants which he is so often called on to render. The short-term Pansa monk can only manage a few chants, at best, during his three- month residence.

Not only must monks memorize the language of the chants, but they must also learn the appropriate modes of chanting. For not all chants are rendered in the same mode.

In *Thai Buddhism, Its Rites and Activities,* Kenneth Wells described seven modes of chanting, of which the most frequently heard is *Sanyoga*, "low-pitched, slow and sustained." Another is *Magadha*, staccato and recitative, used by the Thammayut monks. A third is *Sarabhanna*, high-pitched, slow, mournful, used at inauspicious occasions such as immediately after death. There is a fourth mode, used when four monks chant, rapid and staccato. There is a "melodic and gay form, done with mixed voices, treble and bass"; and a sixth form used with prose, and a seventh suitable for *Suttas*.

A new monk can learn the words of the chants by

reading texts but only by listening to senior monks performing them can he learn to chant them with the proper tunes, rhythms, and intonations. It takes a long time — several months — merely to learn the basic chants, and it takes years to learn the major chants in the monastic repertoire. A monk who is accomplished in chants is indeed to be admired. Those monks who know all the chants — older monks who have spent many years studying them — are deservedly venerated.

Monastic fans are used by monks in some of their chanting ceremonies. These are not conventional fans used for cooling. They are ecclesiastical fans to be held in front of the monk's face and eyes in order to block out any visual distractions while he is chanting, and further to symbolize his apartness, his detachment.

The head of the fan may be made of silk, wool or brocade, and may be beautifully and artistically embroidered. The handle of the fan is usually wooden, except in the cases of old fans whose handles were made of ivory (before use of ivory was declared illegal). The height of the fan is such that when held with its base on the floor its head will be in front of the monk's face when he is seated with his legs crossed.

A monk's fan may indicate his hierarchical rank, in that monks of official status carry fans of different forms and colors and ornamentations appropriate to their status. Except for their fans, since all monks wear similar robes, there is no way of knowing whether a monk is a newly ordained one, an ecclesiastical official, an abbot, or even the Supreme Patriarch. Only a very knowledgeable individual can tell the differences denoted by the fans.

In *Popular Buddhism in Siam* by Phya Anuman Rajadhon, the distinguished Thai scholar wrote that a monk's fan "may be used on five special occasions only", when chanting the three refuges and the five precepts, when a recitation begins, when expressing formal thanks, when taking a robe laid on a coffin, and when chanting certain sacred formulas at cremations.

The Westerner who hears chanting[20] in a temple or on a merit-making occasion does not understand the words but sometimes senses the overall intention of the chants from the context in which they are heard: sermons, blessings, teachings, dedications. The Thai Buddhist layperson, on the other hand, invariably understands the intentions of the chants and a few — scholars or former monks — even understand the Pali words. All Thais understand the three chants which are intoned by a monk at the start of worship services and ceremonies, and are then repeated by the laypersons present:

The first is the *Namo: Namo Tassa Bhagavato Arahato Samma Sambuddhassa*, which pays homage to the Buddha and may be translated, "Homage to the Exalted One, the *Arahant*, the One Perfectly Enlightened by Himself". Monks always chant these words when they begin their meditations,

---

[20] Westerners may be dismayed by what appears to be the occasional lack of attention on the part of laypersons when monks are chanting or conducting worship services in the temple. Ordinarily, laypersons will sit in attitudes of respect, with legs to one side, with hands in the *wai* position, but they may also occasionally talk to their neighbors, may smoke, and may get up to move around, especially when a chant is of long duration, thirty-minutes or longer. This is not to be regarded as a lack of respect, and the monks do not regard it as such. Informality is a Thai way of life, even in the temple. Moreover, the mere act of hearing monks chanting — even though not actually listening —is believed by Buddhists to be a way of earning merit.

their private services, and their monastic rituals, as well as in public ceremonies.

The second is the Three Refuges chant — *Buddham saranam gacchami...Dhammam saranam gacchami... Sangham saranam gacchami.* "I go to the Buddha for refuge. I go to the *Dhamma* for refuge. I go to the *Sangha* for refuge." (By reciting the Three Refugees three times consecutively one attests that one is a Buddhist.)

The third is the Five Precepts chant which, after it has been repeated by the laypersons present, concludes with a monk chanting words that mean in effect, "You have taken the Three Refuges and the Five Precepts for your own welfare. Guard them well, be mindful, and make an effort."

CHAPTER TWENTY-FOUR

MEDITATION, GENERAL

Morality, meditation, and wisdom are the elements of the Eightfold Path through which a Buddhist seeks to attain the goal of enlightment and *nirvana*.

Rare is the Buddhist layperson who manages to live a life of inflexible morality, who does not violate the five lay precepts in one way or another — through improper sexual conduct, through mendacity, through the use of intoxicants or drugs. Rare is the layperson who meditates regularly and consistently. Rare is the layperson who has the wisdom to break the fetters of greed, anger and delusion and to appreciate fully the three Characteristics of Existence, impermanence, no-self, and suffering.

The Buddha knew that the path is hard to follow, especially for the layperson, and that it may take many lifetimes before an individual will have achieved the "perfections" to follow the path successfully. He said, in effect, "It is difficult but try! Don't waste the opportunity you have in this lifetime. Be diligent. Make the effort. Try!" He also acknowledged that the diligent layperson may advance further in the path than the monk who lacks self-control and energy.

In establishing the *Sangha*, the Buddha created conditions under which the self-controlled and energetic monk might follow the path more effectively and more successfully than the layperson.

One of the conditions is that in the monastery a monk must observe the disciplines of the *Patimokkha* — morality, total morality, ethical conduct without the slightest deviation.

Another condition is that in the monastery a monk has the time and the opportunity — free from the distractions of family life or business pursuits — to study *Dhamma*, to learn the *suttas*, the discourses of the Buddha, to read the *Tripitaka* of the Buddhist canon, to benefit from the teachings of the elders, and to meditate in solitude.

The Buddha said that the *bhikkhu* must be perfectly trained in the moral rules, must keep his senses restrained, must have acquired mindfulness and self-possession, and be contented, that these qualities are the prerequisites for effective meditation. In the monastery a monk can train himself in these qualities so that he can obtain the benefits of meditation, the very heart of the monastic life.

A monk's meditation practice differs from that of a layperson's. The lay meditator usually observes one or both of the two forms of Buddhist meditation — *samatha* and *vipassana*. For a layperson who meditates consistently the objective of *samatha* meditation is to calm the mind and develop concentration, and of *vipassana* meditation to sharpen one's intellect through total, alert awareness of oneself and one's own nature. For a monk the objectives and the forms of meditation include these but also go far beyond.

Forty different kinds of meditation were taught by the Buddha to his monastic disciples, and are listed and described in the *Visuddhimagga* ,"The Path of Purification".

Ten are known as *kasinas*, devices for meditating on

earth, water, fire, air, the colors of blue, yellow, red, white, and on light and limited space. These are infrequently practiced.

Ten are meditations on the "foulness of corpses": the bloated corpse, the livid, the festering, the cut up, the gnawed, the scattered, the hacked and scattered, the bleeding, the worm-infested, and the skeletal bones. These too are infrequently practiced these days. In the Buddha's time charnel houses, where corpses could be seen, were common, and these meditations were practiced. (In some monasteries the practice persists these days, with skeletons used for monastic meditation.)

Four meditations are on the "immaterial states": boundless space, boundless consciousness, nothingness, neither perception nor non-perception.

There is a meditation on the "repulsiveness of nutriment", and one on the "defining of the four elements".

The most commonly practised of the monastic meditations are described as "recollection" meditations" — recollection of the Buddha, the *Dhamma*, the *Sangha*, of virtue, generosity, the *devas*, death, foulness of body, and the breathing meditation (which is the meditation most highly recommended by the Buddha and most frequently practised by monks, as well as by laypersons) — and those described as "divine abidings": meditations on loving-kindness, compassion, sympathetic joy, and equanimity.

Not all meditations, the Buddha said, are suitable for all monks. Suitability depends, he said, on an individual monk's temperament: whether it is a greedy temperament, a hating, deluded, faithful, intelligent, or speculative temperament, or various combinations thereof. A senior monk, a "good friend", is best able to determine a junior's temperament and thus to recommend appropriate meditations accordingly, a procedure that was followed in former times more so than now.

In some monasteries today senior monks, meditation masters, do attempt to determine the temperaments of the monks whom they instruct; however, regardless of temperamental dispositions, all monks are required to practice the "protective acts of meditation": those appropriate to the elimination of lust (meditation on the foulness of the body[21]), to the elimination of fear of death (the death meditation), to the elimination of selfishness, anger and hatred (the loving-kindness, compassion, and sympathetic-joy meditations), to the elimination of stressful imbalance (the mindfulness of breathing meditation); and meditation on the wisdom and excellence of the Buddha.

---

[21] Contemplation of the foulness of the body is intended to induce equanimity regarding the body, not aversion.

CHAPTER TWENTY-FIVE

MEDITATION IN PRACTICE

Meditation, as taught by the Buddha, can be practiced in any one of the four postures — sitting, walking, standing, or lying still — but always in accordance with the manner and format prescribed by him. I have chosen — because of its clarity, its relevance, and its therapeutic nature, and because I hope all my readers may find it edifying — to present in detail the format of the meditation on mindfulness of death.

The meditator should begin by thinking, "Death will take place; life will be interrupted." Then the meditator should contemplate death in these ways:

Death is inevitable for whatever is born. Like a murderer with a poised sword, death waits from the moment of birth.

Death is the final ruining of life's success. All health ends in sickness, all youth ends in ageing, all life ends in death.

Death comes to all despite their fame, their great merit, their great strength, their supernormal power, their great understanding, despite their even having been Buddhas. "If they fell into death's power, what can be said of those like me?"

Death comes to the "worms" which have shared our

body, the bacteria which are born, grow old, and die with the body.

Death is reflective of the frailty of life.

Death is unpredictable; it can come at any time.

Death limits what is the short extent of human life.

In the description of the monastic death meditation in the *Visuddhi Magga* the following verses from various scriptures are included:

"The nights and days keep slipping by
As life keeps dwindling steadily
Till mortals' span, like water pools
In failing rills, is all used up."

"The dewdrop on the blade of grass
Vanishes when the sun comes up;
Such is a human span of life."

"As though huge mountains made of rock
So vast they reached up to the sky
Were to advance from every side,
Grinding beneath them all that lives,
So age and death roll over all,
Warriors, monks, merchants and craftsmen,
The outcastes and the scavengers,
Crushing all beings, sparing none...
No strategy, no riches serve to beat them off."

The death meditation is intended to stimulate energy here and now, and to prepare one to face the inevitable without fear.

The Buddha said, this human life span is short. There is a new life to be gone to. There are profitable deeds to be done, and there is the life of purity to be led, so that one may induce a better rebirth, or experience Enlightenment. Mindfulness of death, he said, summons self improvement. One who is mindful of death is constantly diligent, overcomes attachment to life, avoids accumulation of possessions, has a growing perception of impermanence, of *dukkha*, and of the absence of a permanent, abiding self.

Some monastic meditations (described in the preceding chapter) are intended for the cultivation of the monk's character — to clear his mind of lust, hatred, slothfulness, of worries and restlessness, and of skepticism. Others rid him of his attachment to the total physical self and the attachment to ego. Others bring him an awareness of the impermanence of all things. All monastic meditations, directly or indirectly, have insight-wisdom as their goal.

Indeed, the ultimate purpose of meditation is to transform the *Dhamma*, which one may have partially absorbed intellectually through reading or through listening to a teacher, into direct **intuitive** perception, full absorption, and complete understanding — in short, insight-wisdom.

Meditation brings many rewards. For the layperson it calms the mind, induces serenity, and heightens awareness; and for the exceptional layperson, the devoted, consistent meditator, it leads to partial, or even in rare instances, total insight-wisdom. For the monk, meditation can bring all these rewards, and more. It brings what are known as *jhanas*.

A *jhana* is a state of inner absorption (sometimes described improperly as trance-like) brought on by deep meditation. Few laypersons experience *jhana*, in that their meditations are of short duration, perhaps fifteen to thirty minutes. The monk meditates for extended periods,

sometimes for hours on end. He has trained himself to enter
into the meditative process more easily, to penetrate it more
deeply and more quickly. And so he can — but not always,
and not all monks can do so at all — attain *jhana*.

The concept of *jhana* is very difficult for even the most
knowledgeable Buddhist to comprehend fully. For the
following clarifications of *jhana* I have turned to Alexandra
David-Neel's explanation in *Buddhism: Its Doctrines & Its
Methods*, although expressed in my own words:

In the first level of *jhana* the meditator is free of lust,
anger, indifference, agitation, and doubt. In the second, the
meditator experiences enthusiasm and joy, and achieves
inner peace and single-mindedness. In the third, the
meditator goes beyond enthusiasm to clairvoyant
consciousness. In the fourth, the meditator has achieved
total serenity, one-pointedness of mind, and equanimity.
The Buddha said that a lay meditator may attain the first
three *jhanas*, but only with great difficulty the fourth.
Indeed, there are four additional advanced states of jhana
reached perhaps only by those in or near the state of
*Arahant*ship[22]. (I have been told by monk scholars and
teachers that the Westerner newly introduced to Buddhism
should not worry about whether he or she understands or

---

[22] In Theravada Buddhism an *Arahant* is one who has traveled the
path and reached the goal of enlightenment. In Mahayana such an
individual is called a *Bodhisattva* (Sanskrit), but whereas an *Arahant*
has attained *nirvana*, a *Bodhisattva*, out of compassion for mankind,
remains in the cycle of deaths and rebirths in order to assist other
human beings to achieve enlightnment. This is one of the major
differences between Theravada and Mahayana Buddhism. (Note
also that in Pali a *Bodhisatta* is a Buddha-to- be, as Gotama was
before his full enlightenment.)

attains *jhana* in meditation; it is a needless complexity in one's practice.)

In the chapter on the *Patimokkha*, it was noted that one of the four most grave offences a monk can commit, so grave as to require expulsion from the *Sangha*, is to claim having attained superior, supernormal states, such as *Arahant*ship. Little is known, therefore, regarding the attainment of the state of *Arahant* — which is mostly attained by monks, and, indeed, even by very few monks — since they are forbidden to talk about it.

Enlightenment, the state attained by an *Arahant* was, however, explained by the Buddha. It is the state one attains, the Buddha said, when one has cast off the Ten Fetters (the erroneous mental conceptions and desires) that bind one to an ignorant way of living.

When one casts off three of the ten — the illusion of self, mental vacillation or doubt, and attachment to external rites and ceremonies (as substitutes for internal, personal practice of the *Dhamma*) as the essence of religion — one is on the way to enlightenment, and is called a "Stream-Enterer". It may only take seven more lifetimes, or fewer, for that person to attain the state of enlightenment.

When one casts off the first three plus the next two fetters — sensual desires (or delusions of the senses) and ill-will (hatred or aversion) — one is much farther along on the path to enlightenment, and is called a "Once-Returner". One more lifetime is all it will take to reach enlightenment.

When one casts off the foregoing five fetters plus the next two — desire for existence in the world of forms (sentient beings) and desire for existence in the formless worlds (the worlds of gods, *devas*) — one is on the verge of enlightenment, a "Non-Returner". This is the highest state one generally can attain.

Finally, however, when one casts off all the foregoing seven fetters plus the last three — conceit, restlessness, and ignorance (delusion, or lack of insight-wisdom) — one is enlightened, an *Arahant*. The *Arahant* has attained enlightenment or *nirvana* in this lifetime and will at death go on to what is known as *parinirvana*, eternal peace.

Enlightenment and *nirvana* are the goals of the dedicated monk. Meditation, because it cultivates calm and insight-wisdom, accelerates the attainment of these goals, which is why the dedicated monk spends hours every day, day after day, night after night, meditating.

CHAPTER TWENTY-SIX

EXCERPTS FROM THE BUDDHA'S DISCOURSES ABOUT MONKS AND THE MONASTIC LIFE

The monk controls his hands, his feet, his speech. He is well controlled, he delights in his inner control, he is solitary, he is content.

The monk controls his tongue, speaks with wisdom, is not proud, understands cause and effect, knows the *Dhamma*. His speech is sweet as honey.

The monk follows the *Dhamma* and never varies from it.

The monk does not disdain what he is given, does not envy what others are given, because a monk who is disdainful or envious cannot attain meditative serenity.

The monk does not identify himself with "self", does not seek what is unattainable and does not grieve over it.

The monk lives ever in loving-kindness, he is serene in his faith.

The monk who has escaped the first five fetters is one who has "forded the flood".

The monk who has gone to a "lonely place" and who has a serene mind and who perceives the *Dhamma* deeply in his heart experiences a joy no person can otherwise know.

The monk who is serene in body, speech, mind, and heart, and who has renounced worldly desires — he is truly peaceful.

The monk who understands the concept of impermanence, of the rising and falling, the coming and going, of
all physical attributes and of all things — knows the joy of
deathlessness.

The monk who aspires to insight-wisdom guards his
senses, is content, is restrained under the *Patimokkha*, and
keeps the noble company of monks whose lives are pure
and whose minds are keen.

The monk, even the young monk, who is devoted to the
Buddha, the *Dhamma* and the *Sangha* lights up this world as
does the moon in a cloudless sky.

The monk who is full of joy and confidence, and who is
firm in the Buddhist doctrines will attain *nirvana*, the state
of peace, the cessation of all that is mortal and transitory.

****

Meditate, monk, and be not heedless! Do not let sensual
desires befuddle your mind so that you feel the fiery hell
of anguish and cry out, "This is suffering."

He who has no insight-wisdom cannot attain the
rewards of meditation, and he who does not meditate
cannot attain insight-wisdom. Meditation **with** insight-
wisdom brings a monk into the presence of *nirvana*.

Not merely by discipline and vows, nor again by much
learning, not by entering into meditation nor yet by
sleeping apart does a monk earn the bliss of release which
no wordling can know. Monk, be not content as long as
thou has not attained the extinction of desire.

Restraint is good. Restraint of the senses — seeing,
hearing, smelling, tasting, speaking, thinking — is good.
Restraint of body is good. Restraint in **all things** is good.
The monk who is restrained in all things is free of suffering.

Monk, motivate yourself. Examine yourself. Restrain yourself. When you are self-guarded and mindful you live happily.

Monk, you and you alone are your refuge. You and you alone are your pathway.

PART IV

THE GOOD LIFE FOR THE LAYPERSON

CHAPTER TWENTY-SEVEN

THE BUDDHA'S ADVICE TO THE LAYPERSON

As we have read in the preceding chapters, renunciate monks who diligently follow the path — the Buddha called them "warriors", so intense is the monastic struggle — strive with great energy to cast off the ten fetters. That is indeed their purpose for being in the monkhood, where under monastic conditions they have the discipline, the opportunity and the environment for casting off all the fetters and for attaining enlightenment and *nirvana*. That few actually succeed attests to how difficult it is.

If it is so difficult even for the determined monk or nun living under the most favorable conditions for following the path, consider how difficult it is for the layperson to attain enlightenment and *nirvana*. In fact, is it even **possible**?

In the definition of *nirvana* given in *A Popular Dictionary of Buddhism* by Christmas Humphreys, *nirvana* "is attainable in this life by right aspiration, purity of life, and elimination of egoism."

Lay Buddhists, however, do not realistically expect in this lifetime to attain enlightenment or *nirvana*. They can however strive to become "Stream-enterers", and, with great effort, "Once-returners". They do so by practicing morality in their daily lives; by avoiding evil and by doing good, by purifying the heart through mindfulness, self-control, restraint, and the habit of daily meditation. They earn merit through their good deeds and exemplary behavior, thus accumulating good *karma* conducive to propitious rebirth.

In short, the diligent Buddhist layperson attempts to live what the Buddha described as the good life. And just as he prescribed precise rules of conduct and behavior for monks to help them better pursue their goal, he also provided advice and instruction to laypersons to help them pursue the good life.

When one considers that the Buddha's discourses on the good life for the layperson were delivered some two thousand five hundred years ago one can only marvel at their relevance today. They derive from his teachings on morality, and they cover virtually every aspect of everyday life. Though some today may regard them as homiletic and idealistic, those who follow the path try as best they can to behave as the Buddha recommended, remembering that the Buddha never commanded, "You must"; instead he said, "Try".

What the Buddha said is transcribed below for the most part in his words, as translated in various books of the Pali canon, and modified only in some instances by me for better contemporary comprehension.

ON FAMILY BEHAVIOR

In a loving family the home will be like a flower garden. Family discord is like a storm that plays havoc with the garden. When family discord arises do not blame others, but rather examine your own motives, attitudes, and behavior. Even a small misunderstanding, if allowed to develop into serious discord, can bring on family misfortune and disaster. Guard against even the smallest misunderstandings in family life.

ON CHILDREN AND PARENTS

Children should be attentive to their parents' needs. They should not squander their parents' wealth. They should provide for their parents in their old age. They should perform the funeral rites for their parents.

Parents should discipline their children — (discipline in its meanings of teaching and training) — to avoid bad behavior. They should provide their children with good education. They should see to it that they marry into good families. They should pass on their assets to their children.

Heads of families should build economic security through acquiring sufficient wealth by just and righteous means. They should spend liberally but prudently on behalf of themselves, their family, their relatives, their friends, and on deeds which accumulate merit. They should remain free from debt.

ON HUSBANDS AND WIVES

Husbands should accord their wives courtesy, respect, and honor (which, of course, wives should reciprocate). They should be loving and faithful. They should give their wives authority. They should make life secure and comfortable for their wives. They should make their wives happy by giving them clothing and jewelry.

Wives should manage the household. They should be hospitable and gracious to guests, friends, relatives, and husband's employees. They should be loving and faithful.

They should be thrifty and non-profligate with their husband's earnings. They should be alert, intelligent, and efficient.

(There is little here to upset today's liberated woman, except perhaps "manage the household". The Buddha might have amended that had he been able to forecast the contemporary status of women.)

ON FRIENDS, RELATIVES, AND NEIGHBORS

They should behave with hospitality and generosity toward one other. They should speak gently and cordially. They should see to one another's welfare. They should not be quarrelsome or disputatious. They should offer a helping hand in times of need. They should not abandon those in difficult straits.

ON FALSE FRIENDS AND TRUE FRIENDS

A false friend is one who exploits you financially, who takes from you and does not give in return, who is selfish, who is overly complimentary, who flatters excessively, who agrees with whatever you say or do, who praises you to your face and slanders you behind your back, who makes excuses when asked to do you a favor.

A true friend is one who gives you sound advice, who is sympathetic, who is steadfast, who protects you when you need defense, protects your property when you are negligent, shelters you in times of distress, helps in every way possible to increase your fortune, who confides in you and in whom you may confide, who discourages your vices and encourages your virtues, who shares your sorrows, rejoices in your joys, rebukes those who speak ill of you, commends those who speak well of you, who would make the ultimate sacrifice if needed to save your life.

ON TEACHERS AND PUPILS

Pupils should be respectful and obedient. They should attend to their teacher's needs, if any. They should study diligently.

Teachers should train and mould shape their pupils properly. They should teach them well. They should introduce pupils to their friends. They should try to provide security for their pupils and to find them employment when their schooling is over.

ON EMPLOYERS AND EMPLOYEES

Employers should assign to their employees only tasks which their employees have the physical strength and the mental capability of handling. They should pay adequate wages and should provide for medical needs. They should give their employees vacations and bonuses.

Employees should work energetically and not shirk their responsibilities. They should be honest and never cheat their employers. They should be forthright and attentive. They should speak well of their employers.

(The Buddha's time was one of masters and servants. And, by the way, this is still true in countries like Thailand where households, even of modest means, employ servants. One of the Buddha's admonitions to employee-servants was: arise before your masters do, retire after they do. This was regarded — still is in Thailand — as not being exploitative but rather as contributing to the orderliness and well-being of the household.)

The Buddha said further: Those who cheat in business, those who swindle or deceive, hurt themselves as well as those whom they cheat, swindle or deceive, for the deeds and misdeeds of people *(karma)* remain within themselves.

And he gave this additional advice for the business person: one-fourth of your income should be spent on current needs, one-fourth should be saved for future needs, two-fourths should be reinvested in your business.

ON MALE BEHAVIOR TOWARD A FEMALE

A male should speak to a female with a pure heart. If she is old he should regard her as lovingly as he would his mother. If she is older than he, he should regard her as respectfully as he would an older sister. If she is younger than he, he should regard her as considerately as he would a younger sister. If she is a child he should treat her deferentially and politely.

ON SOCIAL BEHAVIOR

Abstain from backbiting and slander, from language that may cause hatred, enmity, disunity, disharmony. Abstain from language that is harsh, rude, impolite, malicious, abusive. Abstain from idle, foolish babble. Abstain from gossip. If you cannot say anything friendly, benevolent, meaningful, and useful, keep a noble silence.

Be tolerant with the intolerant. Be mild with the violent; even if you have power over others, yet be gentle, especially with the weak. Be patient, restrained, compassionate.

Be free from greed among the greedy. Do not seek to gain by the loss of others.

Instead of finding fault in others, look to your own

misdeeds. Do not judge harshly. See both sides, and judge fairly.

Do not deceive nor despise nor wish harm to another person. Meet hatred with kindness, evil with goodness, greed with generosity, lies with truth.

A person's position in society is not determined by birth, but by worth, not by descent but by conduct and character. Try to treat all people alike. You will understand others insofar as you understand yourself. You will sympathize with others when you realize that they experience the same suffering *(dukkha)* as you. Love others as you love yourself. Protecting yourself through mindfulness you protect others; protecting others through kindness and patience you protect yourself.

ON RELIGIONS

Do not decry, depreciate, or condemn the religions of others. Honor whatever in them is worthy of honor. Listen, be curious, be willing to understand the doctrines of others.

ON BENEFICIAL ACTIVITIES

These things, the Buddha taught, benefit all persons:

In your job, trade, craft, profession—be skilled, efficient, earnest, energetic, knowledgeable. Protect your income. Spend in proportion to your income, not too much, not too little. Do not be avaricious. Do not hoard wealth. Do not be extravagant, but live within your means.

Associate with good friends who are faithful, learned, virtuous, liberal, intelligent; who will help you along the right path and away from evil.

Have faith and confidence in moral, spiritual, and

intellectual values.

Practise charity and generosity without attachment to wealth or craving for wealth.

ON WEALTH

There are four requirements for accumulating wealth: Determined energy, conservation of what is earned, living simply, associating with good people.

When you have accumulated wealth, do not consider it as wholly your own. Share with others. Set aside some for the needs of your community and your nation. Set aside some for the needs of the religious teachers. Save some for emergencies.

And always remember that the greatest wealth is contentedness.

ON CHARITY AND GENEROSITY

Cultivate wholesomeness by giving useful things to those who are in need: food, clothing, money. Be charitable even if you are poor, but not to the detriment of your own welfare.

A truly virtuous person helps those in need purely out of compassion, not out of hope for personal gain or the accumulation of merit, and without caring whether one's generosity is seen or acknowledged.

ON UNETHICAL CONDUCT

The Buddha counseled all laypersons to avoid all manifestations of unethical conduct, to wit: hostility and malice toward others, hypocrisy, deceitfulness, stealing the property of others, defrauding creditors by denying that debts are owed them, bearing false witness, adultery, failure to support elderly parents.

He counseled them to avoid offending, by words or blows, any members of the family, giving false advice, failure to return another's hospitality, making others angry.

He urged them to reject avarice, envy, cunning, cruelty, harsh language.

He bade them to undertake the rules of training in the practice of the Five Precepts.

ON HOSTILITY

Hatred cannot be appeased by hatred. Hatred cannot be appeased by thinking that person abused me, beat me, defeated me, robbed me. Do not hate those who hate you. Hatred can only be appeased by love.

Do not speak harshly to others; they will only answer harshly. Angry speech brings trouble. Bear insult without making an angry reply. The just man does not resort to winning by violence.

ON INTEMPERANCE

The dangers of heedless intoxication, the Buddha said, are: squandering of wealth, argumentativeness, risk of illness, risk of scandal, rejection by society, and weakening of the facilities.

ON THE SQUANDERING OF WEALTH

The following activities, the Buddha said, lead to the dissipation of wealth: indulging in intoxicants, carousing (literally,spending the night wandering about the town), night-clubbing (literally, haunting fairs), gambling, keeping bad company, and idleness.

ON IDLENESS

The idle person finds many excuses to avoid working: It is too hot to work. It is too cold. It is too early to work. It is too late. I have not eaten enough to work. I have eaten too much.

Such a person goes through life neglecting duty and responsibility, failing to acquire assets, and failing to preserve whatever assets may already have been possessed.

If something is to be done, do it vigorously.

ON CRIMINAL THEFT

The cause is poverty. Punishment of wrong-doers is futile. Improved economic conditions are essential to the eradication of criminal theft.

(In the Buddha's time there was no white-collar crime, no embezzlement crime by the rich and powerful, no organized crime like that of today's Mafia. Thus, poverty, he said, was the source of crime.)

ON THOSE WHO GOVERN

The Buddha proposed ten rules for those who govern. These rules were addressed to the kings of his time, and they apply today to heads of states, political leaders, legislative, judicial, or executive leaders, to any one who holds public trust and is responsible for the public good:

1. Be liberal, generous, charitable. Do not use your

position to accumulate wealth and property.

2. Obey the five precepts: do not destroy life, lie, steal, engage in illicit sex, use intoxicants heedlessly.

3. Make your paramount concern the welfare of your people.

4. Govern with integrity. Do not deceive your people.

5. Be kind, gentle, and genial.

6. Lead a simple life, self-controlled, non-sybaritic.

7. Be free of hatred toward anybody.

8. Promote peace and non-violence.

9. Be patient, tolerant, forbearing.

10. Do not oppose the will of the people.

(Should these instructions be included in the oath of office taken by all those in government today?)

ON THE TEN SOURCES OF HAPPINESS

1. To serve the wise and to honor those who deserve honor.

2. To dwell in a pleasant land, to have done good works in a former birth, to nurture right desires.

3. To cultivate clarity of mind, a pleasant manner of speech,learning, self-mastery.

4. To support one's parents, to cherish one's spouse and children, to follow a peaceful calling.

5. To give alms, to live with uprightness, to help one's kin, to act beyond reproach.

6. To abhor and cease from evil, to abstain from intoxicants, to persist in well-doing.

7. To be reverent and humble, to be content and grateful, to study the *Dhamma*.

8. To be patient and gentle, to keep the company of peaceful, non-violent persons, to speak properly of spiritual

matters.

9. To be self-restrained, to know the Four Noble Truths, to realize *nirvana*.

10. To develop equanimity, to avoid yielding to grief or to passion.

****

Many laypersons will regard the Buddha's prescriptions for the good life as too difficult for them to heed. But as the Buddha said when Mara tried to dissuade him from teaching *Dhamma*, "There are some who will understand", he might have said about his advice to laypersons, "There are some who will heed." Those who do are the ones who try most diligently to follow the path to enlightenment.

A BUDDHIST'S CREED

I will conduct myself with ethical rectitude in all my actions, all my thoughts.

I will treat all people, all sentient beings, with sympathetic understanding, with compassion, with loving-kindness.

I will resist anger.

I will desist from greed.

I will cultivate mental tranquility.

I will meditate; I will be mindful of all my actions, all my thoughts.

I will reject egoistic desire, all notions of a unity called self, all notions of permanence.

I will not regret the past nor fret about the future.

I will develop equanimity; I will not allow myself to exult in my good fortune or to despair in my bad fortune.

I will strive to the best of my ability to follow the path to enlightenment.

GENERAL GLOSSARY

Abhidhamma (Pali) Advanced Dhamma. Philosophical and psychological analyses of the sermons. The third division of the Tipitaka (q.v.)

Abhisamacara (Pali) The rules of training and propriety for monks.

Achaan (Thai) or **Ajahn** Teacher

Anapanasati (Pali) The meditation practice in which one concentrates on breathing in and breathing out. (Literally, mindfulness of breathing)

Anatta (Pali); **Anatman** (Skt) The concept of 'no-self' — there is no absolute soul or self, one of the Three Characteristics of Existence.

Anicca (Pali) Impermanence; another of the Three Characteristics of Existence.

Apatti (Pali) Offences; violations of the monastic rules

Arahant; or **Arhat** (Skt) or **Arahat** (Pali) In Theravada, one who has attained enlightenment. In Mahayana, **Bodhisattva** (q.v.)

Asala Bucha (Thai) Buddhist holy day in the eighth lunar month

Bhikkhu (Pali); **Bhikshu** (Skt) A Buddhist monk; (literally, a mendicant). Feminine equivalent is **Bhikkhuni, Bhikshuni**

Bo tree A fig tree like that under which the Buddha attained enlightenment

Bodhgaya The town in northern India where the Buddha attained enlightenment

Bodhisatta In Theravada, a Buddha-to-be; in Mahayana, **Bodhisattva** — one who has attained enlightenment but is postponing entrance to Nirvana in order to aid all fellow beings toward salvation

Buddha 'The Enlightened One', Siddartha Gotama's title after he attained *Nirvana*

Buddham saranam gacchami (Pali) To the Buddha I go for refuge

Chedi (Thai); **Stupa** (Skt) A mound or tower serving as a Buddhist shrine; a symbol of the Buddha

Dek wat (Thai) Temple boy; a young layperson who assists the monks and, often, attends the temple school

Devas (Skt) Celestial beings; gods; they can be benign or malign

Dhamma (Pali), **Dharma** (Skt) Many meanings: law, condition, phenomenon, event, reality, the truth, and, most commonly, the doctrine and teachings of the Buddha

Dhammam saranam gacchami (Pali) To the *Dhamma* I go for refuge

Dhammapada (Pali) "The Path of Truth"; the collection of 423 verses spoken by the Buddha on various occasions

Dip (Thai) Unripe, raw, immature

Dosa (Pali) Aversion, one of the Three Defilements, along with *Lobha* and *Moha* (q.v.)

Dukkha (Pali) The suffering, pain, and unsatisfactory nature and conditions of existence. One of the Three Characteristics of Existence. The First Noble Truth.

Farang (Thai) Foreigner

Five Aggregates (see **Khandas**)

Five Precepts The Buddhist code of moral behavior for laypersons. (See text)

Four Noble Truths There is suffering,Dukkha; the cause of suffering; the elimination of suffering; the Noble Eightfold Path. (See text)

Jhana (Pali); **Dhyana** (Skt) Deep state of meditative absorption

Karma(Skt); **Kamma** (Pali) The Buddhist concept of cause and effect that transcends individual lifetimes

Kasina (Pali) A type of meditation where one concentrates on a an object like a colored disc and then recalls the image as a means of developing calm and concentration to quiet the mind

Khandas (Pali); **Skandhas** (Skt) The five aggregates that make up the human being: body, feelings, perceptions, predispositions, and consciousness

Khao Pansa (Thai) The start of the three month 'Buddhist Lent' during the rains season

Khuti or **kuti** (Thai) The modest living quarters of a monk

Lobha (Pali) Greed or covetousness

Luang phi (Thai) Venerable brother; **Luang pho**, venerable father; **Luang phu**, venerable grandfather. (Respectful forms of address which Thai laypersons use in addressing monks.)

Mae-chii (Thai) A Buddhist woman renunciate in Thailand, referred to as a nun

Mahamangala Sutta A sutta in which the Buddha described the ten sources of happiness for a layperson

Mahanikai The Thai monastic order to which most Thai monks belong

Mahayana Buddhism The form of Buddhism practiced in Tibet, China, Japan, Mongolia and Korea. Also known as the 'Greater Vehicle'

Makha Bucha (Thai) A Buddhist holy day in the third lunar month

Metta (Pali) Universal love

Naga (Skt) A kind of serpent, a mythical creature in Buddhist lore; also, a candidate for ordination

Moha (Pali) Delusion

Namo Tassa Bhagavato Arahato Summa Sumbud-dhassa (Pali) Homage to the Exalted One, the Arahant, the One Perfectly Enlightened by Himself (the Buddha)

Nirvana (Skt); **Nibbana** (Pali) The ultimate goal of Buddhist practice: enlightenment; release from the round of birth and rebirth

Noble Eightfold Path The eight principles of Buddhist practice: Right Action, Right Speech, Right Livelihood, Right Effort, Right Mindfulness, Right Concentration, Right View, Right Thought

Om mani padme hum A well-known Tibetan Buddhist mantra, used during and for meditation. "Hail to the jewel in the lotus." (See text for more)

Pali The ancient religious language of India in which the Theravadan Buddhist teachings were first written down. (Sanskrit was the ancient language of Mahayana Buddhist teachings.)

Panna (Pali); **Prajna** (Skt) Wisdom

Pansa (Thai); **Vassa** (Pali) The rainy season, the three-month period of monastic retreat

  Khao Pansa, entering *Pansa*; **Ok Pansa**, leaving *Pansa*

Parinirvana (Skt) Final and complete nirvana; attained at death, as in the death of the Buddha

Patimokkha (Pali); **Patimomoksha** (Skt) The 227 monastic disciplinary rules, sometimes called precepts

Pavarana (Pali) A monastic ceremony in which at the start of *Pansa* all monks in a monastery gather to vow that they will live together harmoniously

Pindapata (Thai) The monks' early morning round of walking for food and alms in the neighborhood of their monasteries

Pra (Thai) or **Phra** Honorific for a monk

Sai sin (Thai) Holy thread

Sala (Thai) Open-sided assembly hall

Samatha (Pali and Skt) A type of meditation where one tries to ignore all sensory diversions, as differentiated from *'Vipassana'*(q.v.) meditation where one tries to be aware of them

Samsara (Pali and Skt) The cycle of death and rebirth for those who have not attained *Nirvana*

Sangha (Pali and Skt) The Buddhist monastic order; also describes the community (togetherness) of monks and laity

Sangham saranam gacchami (Pali) To the Sangha I go refuge

Sanuk (Thai) Fun, enjoyment

Sila (Pali and Skt) The practice of moral virtues; Buddhist ethics

Sima (Pali) Stones that mark the consecrated grounds of the *uposatha* (see below)

Songkran (Thai) The traditional Thai New Year; time of the water festival

Suk (Thai) Ripe, finished, mature

Sukkha (Pali) The antithesis of *'dukkha'*; the existence of happiness, joy, achievement, fulfillment and well-being

Sutta(Pali; **Sutra** (Skt) A discourse by the Buddha, or one of his disciples. (Literally, the thread on which jewels are hung)

Tanha (Pali); **Trishna** (Skt) Craving, desire and attachment

— the major hurdles to be overcome in order to attain enlightenment or to become an ethical and moral person.

Tantrayana Buddhism (See Vajrayana Buddhism)

Tantric Esoteric Buddhist practices based on oral transmission rather than written text

Taoism An ancient Chinese philosophy based on the principles of nature and the interplay of opposite forces

Thammayut (Thai) A Thai monastic order founded by King Mongkut, Rama IV; fewer monks belong to it than to the Mahanikai order (q.v.)

Thanka (Tib) A Tibetan religious painted scroll which depicts Buddhist cosmology.

Theravada Buddhism The form of Buddhism practiced in Thailand, Burma, Laos, Cambodia, Sri Lanka, and Nepal. Also known as Hinayana (the 'Lesser Vehicle') and 'The Way of the Elders'.

The Triple Gem, or **The Three Jewels** The Buddha, the *Dhamma* (teachings of the Buddha),and the *Sangha* (the monastic community)

Tipitaka (Pali) or **Tripitaka**. "Three Baskets" of the Theravada Buddhist scriptures: the *Vinaya*, the *Suttas*, and the *Abhidhamma* (the Higher *Dhamma*)

Tot Kathin (Thai) A month-long period of special merit-making for laypersons after *Pansa*, when robes and other gifts are given to monks

Upajjhaya (Pali) Preceptor

Upasampada (Pali) The ceremony of full ordination

Uposatha (Pali); **Bot** (Thai) The most sacrosanct building in a *wat* (q.v.); also the Buddhist holy days of Full Moon, New Moon, and the days equi-distant

Vajrayana Buddhism An esoteric school of Mahayana

Buddhism practiced in Tibet (not Tibetan Buddhism as a whole), also known as the 'Diamond Vehicle'

Vinaya (Pali) The first division of the *Tipitaka* (q.v.); The rules of life, training, and discipline governing the *Sangha*(q.v.)

Vipassana (Pali) A type of meditation that cultivates mental awareness and insight-wisdom

Visuddhi Magga (Pali) "Path of Purification"; title of a classic manual of Buddhist doctrine and meditation written in the 5th century by the monk Buddhagosa

Wat (Thai) A Buddhist temple-monastery

Way of the Elders The name which Theravadans call their form of Buddhism. Theravada Buddhism is also sometimes called 'the Old Wisdom School' since its scriptures are derived from the teachings of the Buddha as recorded in the earliest written texts

BIBLIOGRAPHY

Babbitt, Irving , trans., *The Dhammapada*. New York, New Directions
    Paperbook, 1965

Blofeld, John, *The Tantric Mysticism of Tibet*. New York, E.P. Dutton &
    Co., Inc. 1970

Burtt, E.A. Ed., *The Teachings of the Compassionate Buddha*.
    New York, A Mentor Book, 1955

Ch'en Kenneth K.S., *Buddhism, the Light of Asia*. New York,
    Barron's Educational Series, 1968

Conze, Edward, *Buddhism: Its Essence and Development*. New York,
    Harper Torchbooks, 1975

——————*Buddhist Scriptures*. New York, Penguin Books Ltd., 1959

David-Neel, Alexandra, *Buddhism, Its Doctrines & Its Methods*. New
    York, Avon Discus, 1979

Goddard, Dwight, Ed., *A Buddhist Bible*. Boston, Beacon Press, 1970

Grimm, George, *Buddhist Wisdom: The Mystery of the Self*. Delhi, Motilal
    Banarsidass, 1978

Hamilton-Merritt, Jane, *A Meditator's Diary*. London, Unwin Paper-
    backs, 1986

Humphreys, Christmas, *A Popular Dictionary of Buddhism*. London,
    Curzon Press Ltd., 1962

——————— ed., *The Wisdom of Buddhism*. London, Curzon Press
    Ltd.,1960

Indasara, Wasin, *Theravada Buddhist Principles*. (2 vols.) Bangkok,
    Mahamakut Buddhist University, 1977

Jackson, Peter A., *Buddhadasa: A Buddhist Thinker for the Modern World*.
    Bangkok, The Siam Society, 1988

Jacobson, Nolan Pliny, *Buddhism & The Contemporary World*. Southern
    Illinois University Press, 1983

Jayasuriya, Dr. W. F., *The Psychology & Philosophy of Buddhism: An In-*

troduction to the Abhidhamma. Kuala Lumpur, Buddhist Missionary Society, 1976

Khantipalo, Pra, *Buddhism Explained.* Chiang Mai, Silkworm Books. 1989

──────*The Splendour of Enlightenment: A Life of the Buddha* (2 vols.) Bangkok, Mahamkut Press, 1987

───────(Translator) *The Dhammapada.* Bangkok, Mahamkut Press,1977

──────*Calm and Insight, a Buddhist Manual for Meditators.* London, Curzon Press Ltd., 1981

────── *Pointing to Dhamma.* Bangkok, Mahamkut Press, 1973

Lester, Robert C., *Theravada Buddhism in Southeast Asia.* Ann Arbor, The University of Michigan Press, 1973

Nanamoli, Bhikkhu, (Translator), *The Path of Purification, Visuddhi Magga* by Bhadantacariya Buddhaghosa. Kandy, Buddhist Publication Society, 1979

Paravahera Vajirasana Mahathera, *Buddhist Meditation, in Theory and Practice.* Kuala Lumpur, Buddhist Missionary Society,1962

Rahula, Walpola, *What the Buddha Taught.* Bangkok, HawTrai Foundation, 1990

Rajadhon, Phya Anuman, *Popular Buddhism in Siam.* Bangkok, Thai Inter-Religious Commission for Development & Sathirakases Nagapradipa Foundation

Rhys-Davids, T.W., Buddhism: *A Sketch of the Life and Teachings of Gautama, the Buddha.* Delhi, Indological Book House, 1877 (Note: probably reprinted and available elsewhere)

Ross, Nancy Wilson, *Buddhism: A Way of Life and Thought.* New York, Vintage Books Random House, 1980

Sivaraksa, Sulak, *A Socially Engaged Buddhism.* Bangkok Thai Inter- Religious Commission for Development,1988

Smith, Huston, *The Religions of Man.* New York, Harper & Row,Inc.,1958

Stryk, Lucien, Ed., *World of the Buddha.* New York, Grove Press, Inc., 1982

Sumedho, Ajahn, *Cittaviveka, Teachings from the Silent Mind,* a selection of Dhamma talks, Chithurst Forest Monastery, England.

Suzuki, D. T., *Zen Buddhism.* New York, Anchor Books, Doubleday Company Inc., 1956

Tambiah, S.J., *Buddhism and the Spirit Cults in North-East Thailand.* Cambridge University Press, 1970

Thomas, Edward J. *The Life of the Buddha as Legend and History*. London, Routledge & Kegan Paul, 1948

Upatissa, Arahant, *The Path of Freedom; Vimuttimaga*. Colombo, Dr. D. Roland Weerasuria, 1961

Vajiraranavarorasa, Prince and Supreme Patriarch, *The Entrance to the Vinaya* (3 vols.) Bangkok, Mahamakutarajavidyalaya,1969

———————— *Navakovada: Instructions for Newly-Ordained Bhikkhus and Samaneras*. Bangkok,Mahakutarajavidyalaya, 1971

Venerable Mahasi Sayadaw Agga Maha Pandita, *The Satipatthana Vipassana Meditation*. Rangoon, Department of Religious Affairs, 1979

Venerable Nyanamoli; Pra Khantipalo, Ed., *A Treasury of the Buddha's Discourses* (from the Middle Collection) (3 vols) Bangkok, Mahamakut Press, no date

Wells, Kenneth E., *Thai Buddhism: Its Rites and Activities*. Bangkok, Suriyabun Publishers, 1975

BUDDHIST SCRIPTURES

(For readers who wish to go on to advanced studies of the Buddhist Scriptures themselves — the words of the Buddha and the commentaries — a major library will probably have the following:)

Book of the Discipline (4 vols) I.B. Horner, trans., London, Oxford University Press,

Book of the Gradual Sayings (Anguttara-Nikaya) (5 vols) F.L. Woodward, trans., London, Luzac and Co.

Book of the Kindred Sayings (Samyutta-Nikaya) (5 vols) C.A.F. Rhys-Davids, trans. Vols 1 and 2 and F.L. Woodward, trans. Vols 3,4,5; London, Luzac and Co.

Buddha's Teachings (Sutta-Nipata or Discourse-Collection); Dhammapada Commentary. Chalmers, Lord, ed. and trans., Harvard Oriental Series, vol. 37, Cambridge, Harvard University Press

Collection of the Middle Sayings (Majjhima-Nikaya). (3 vols) I.B. Horner, trans., London. Luzac and Co. (And see above: Venerable Nyanamoli)

Dialogues of the Buddha (3 vols) T.W. Rhys-Davids, trans. Part 1; T.W. and C.A.F. Rhys-Davids, trans. Parts 2 and 3. London, Oxford U. Press

INDEX

(Please note that major topics are also listed in the Table of Contents)